TALES OF ROMANCE IN INDIAN HISTORY AND ART

21 ENHANCING LOVE STORIES OF EMPERORS, KINGS, NAWABS, NIZAMS, ETC...

ROSSLYN ALEXANDER DEAS

ISBN 979-888606469-8

Contents

About The Author *v*

Foreword *vii*

Prologue *ix*

1. Jodha Akbar 1
2. Rama-sita 5
3. Shiva-parvati 10
4. Shajahan-mumtaz Shajahan-mumtaz Mahal 15
5. Bajirao-mastani 18
6. Maharaja Ranjit Singh And Moran Sarkar 22
7. Salim - Anarkali 25
8. Shivaji-saibai 28
9. Quli Qutub Shah And Bhagmati 31
10. Bimbisara And Amrapali 33
11. Raja Man Singh Tomar And Mrignayani 35
12. Rani Padmavati And Raja Ratan Singh 38
13. Emperor Jahangir And Nur Jahan 45
14. Prithviraj Chauhan And Sanyogita 51
15. Aurangzeb And Hirabai 54
16. Rani Roopmati And Sultan Baz Bahadur 59
17. Maharani Gayatri Devi And Maharaja Sawai Man Singh 63
18. Raja Indrajit And Rai Praveen 67
19. Krishna And Rukmini 71
20. Moomal And Mahendra 76
21. Helen Of Troy And Paris 79
22. Romeo And Juliet 84
23. Isabelle And Ferdinand Of Spain 87
24. Cleopatra And Mark Anthony 90

Examples Of Romance In Art 93

About The Author

Ross Deas

Ross wrote his first novel **The MadGamon** at the age of 19 which landed him his first job as a

copywriter in J Walter Thompson, in Mumbai. He continued writing short stories which were published by various newspapers and magazines in India. He moved on to teaching in a school called **TheScholar** from which emanated the **Memorex Education System**, which he wrote and which became a bestseller during 1972-1983 with over 500,000 copies sold. His second book helped sell Bruce Lee's movie, "Enter the Dragon", a book titled **BlackBeltKarate–Itcansavcyourlife,**it sold over 400,000 copies in the 70s. Ross continued writing books like, "**Using the right words**" and "**Success Systems**", based on his success story. He was widely written about during the 70s, 80s and 90s, the most prominent being a Times of India article by Dina Vakil (retired editor), who wrote **Thegospelaccording to St Ross**, which made him well known in India. Another article in Business India, called Ross **"A walking advertisement for Enterprise"** – in a lead story, talking about his various successes.

Ross launched India's first mail order company in 1972, Ross Murarka Inc, an astounding success. He then went on to start a large flower business, **"Love is a Rose"**, an advertising agency "**Headstart**", (which later became "**HeadstartFilms**"), in partnership with his friend. Together, they made "**London Dreams**" the movie, in 2010 featuring Salman Khan and Ajay Devgan.

He bought and later started 2 chemical companies in South India, (**Rosschem Ltd and Tamil Nadu Chemical Products Ltd** – A 700 crore company today). In the 80s and 90s, he was involved in helping the Khaitans of Kolkatta to create the world's biggest Tea Company, namely **George Williamson/Mcloed Russell Ltd.** His love of music, led him to buy into **HMV**, with RP Goenka,(who later bought him out) and saw the launch of **"Disco Deewane"**, selling over a million records making Nazia Hussain, a singing sensation.

Ross also published 3 magazines; "**Beautiful Magazine, Purchase Magazine** (India's first and most successful industrial Magazine), and **Director Magazine"**. He also published India's first stock market newspaper; "**MoneyOpportunities**", that sold over 200,000 copies every week in 3 languages; English, Hindi and Gujarati, taking the stock market up and created thousands of Investors and Shareholders. Business World Magazine called "Money Opportunities", **"Oneofthemostsuccessfulproductsofthe 1980's".** Ross's Company, **Ross Murarka India PVT LTD**, in the 1980's went on to become India's first computer leasing company (in association with DCM) and the first Xerox leasing company (in association with Modi Xerox). He leased India's largest computer in 1983/84 to TATA Steel - Kolkatta. He helped in the turnaround of Binny Textiles – Bangalore, in 1987/88. His company went public in 1984. The share issue being oversubscribed 9 times, making him, at 39 years, one of India's richest "self-made" men.

Ross was a great lover of horses, growing up surrounded by them at the huge home of his English (Doctor) grandmother (Emilia Rose) in Rakjot, his hometown. She brought Ross up, as he lost his mother at the early age of 4. Later on, he went on to become one of India's most successful racehorse owner, becoming a legend in racing and receiving a trophy, "legend in racing", winning 2 Indian Derbies in 1992 & 1999, and was the owner of India's greatest

2 world famous horses; **AstonishandSaddle-up**, who together won many

races in Asia and USA. A serious car accident in 1993 forced Ross to sell his businesses as he was bedridden for almost 2 years with spinal injury problems. However, his spirit was undaunted. He made a comeback with The Millionaire Media Group in London and Dubai, from where, he published almost 26 magazines in different global editions, namely; **Value(UAE),Signature(UAE),BarclaysBankPrestige(Africa),HeritageHotels(UK),Sheraton Hotels – Sojorn (Middle East)** and his own 16 editions of Millionaire Magazines covering the Globe printing and partly selling 18 million copies annually.

On 9th August 1994, Ross was invited to be the "Chief Guest of Honour" at his Alma Mater, St Xavier's College, Bombay, for the 125th Anniversary celebration.

A proud day in his life!

Again in 2006, Ross had a major car accident in Dubai, where he had shifted to in 1996. This accident put him in hospital for a couple of months and he once again, in 2006, he sold his publishing business piecemeal, to various publishers. In 2007, on his way out, leaving Dubai for good, at the airport, he bumped into an old friend, Sushil Ansal of Ansal Properties, Delhi, who asked him to turn back and not take the flight to Bombay, and to market the various Ansal real-estate projects to Indians based in the Middle East. Ross accepted the challenge, stayed on in Dubai, restarted a company called Millionaire Properties. This endeavour was successful till June 2009, having sold crores of Rupees worth of properties for Ansals, Hiranandani, ETA Star, Lokhandwala, creating a buzz, when he sold a whole building of 165 flats in 1 single day in June 2006 - for the Lokhandwala's, a building called **Lady Ratan Manor.** The global crash of December 2008 which ran through to 2009, led to Ross losing most of his fortune he had made in the Middle East, forcing him to sell his Rolls Royce, Mercedes cars, his 2 yachts (Arabella and Friendship), his Jaguar, his Porsche, and many of his (11) homes around the world. Undaunted, Ross at 65, came back to India in 2009 and sold a large property in South India and bounced back partially, only to get involved later, to help make the movie **"London Dreams".** Ross then spent the next couple of years introducing **India's first Portable Solar Lamps** with Eureka Forbes and built himself a garden home in Thailand with that profit, creating a Butterfly Park, an Orchid Park and breeding fish (Siamese Fighters). His stay for a couple of years in Thailand led to him writing 3 books, "**Speak Thai Immediately"** for tourists, "**Speak English Immediately"** for Thai locals, and "**Majestic Thailand"** – a coffee table travel book, aimed at the 30 million tourists who visit Thailand yearly.

"Covid 19 infact" says Ross, "was a boon for me". He got back to writing and his first book, **StopPainGetRelief** was born out of the free clinic he ran at Dadar, Mumbai. This book was soon followed by, **TheGreatMasterminds Series 1-4** together with a game called **Be a Mastermind**. His next book, **Sit Work Lose Weight** – The Constant Motion System, something he had designed, after his accident, to lose the 35 kilos he had put on. He also wrote a book called **Survival – This book can save your life, The Start-Up Upstarts,** which includes a guide to set up a 'start-up' in India and **India's 100 richest men**, a book, together with a **Be a Millionaire** (game), based on the Indian + USA stock markets. In between Ross has scripted 4 novels, **The Dagger of Islam**, **Con-Dom** - an IT love story based in Bangalore, **Sinderella**– a story on the various foreign women who live and work in the call centres of Delhi and his Opus that he is currently working on, namely, **LordMonty'sColonialSaga**which he is aiming at making a series for Netflix/BBC. Now at home thanks to the corona virus, serial entrepreneur Ross, refuses to retire and has gone back to learning to play music on his Casio CT 9000.

"My goal", says Ross, **"is to create music and hymns for God in heaven, design butterflies, tropical fish, birds, orchids, plants, the major loves of my life"**, and about which he is constantly studying. **"I aim to live till 100"**, says Ross, now 76 years old, **"I have only started my journey to heaven right now"**, Ross's love for children led him to run a free school for 220 children in Chennai over the last 20 years, **"Ross English High School"** which sadly he had to sell the school after the 2008 crash. He also supports orphans at Don Bosco. He says, **"Giving and helping people makes me the happiest" – His favourite book, The Bible, is his inspiration.** - Nisha Mavani (Editor)

Foreword

24 Great Love Stories of Emperors, Rajas, Ranis,Nawabs and Nizams

Isthemostcelebratedandyearnedforfeelingbymany.Quiteanotoriousone messingupwitheverybody'slifeLovefromtimeandagainhasbeenportrayedin differentversionsaccordingtopeople'sconvenience.Forsomelovehappensonly oncewithapartner,somefallheadoverheelsandscrewthemselves,somegiveuptheir dreamstobewiththeirlove,somefindloveovercourseoflifeoutofmarriage,some equatelusttolove,somefindcalmnessinlove,somefightbattlesforlove.Theseare prettymuchthekindoflovestoriesfromIndianhistory.

The Love Stories from Indian history withstoodtime.

Howdidtheyfallinloveandhowdidtheymanagetobeinlove? Didtheyremainhappyinloveinspiteoftheoppositionfromthe worldfortheirlove.Orisitbecausetheirlovewastested over time that it became so famous and revered.

Prologue

INTRODUCTION...

EXPRESSIONS OF ROMANTICISM AND RELIGIOUS MIX IN

INDIA-SOME GREAT LOVE STORIES OF INDIAN RULERS

Indiaistrulyalandofdiversity,whereimmortallovestoriescanbefound nexttothelegendarywarstories,wherevaliantkingsfoughtforboththeir kingdomandtheirlove.Nowcomesthequestion;intheoldendayswere Kings (and rulers) allowed to sleep with any woman in their kingdom (includingwomenwhowerealreadymarried)?Itwasn'tlikeanexplicitright. Therewasnolawinanynationstating,"thekingcansleepandhavesex withanyoneofhischoice,"norwasthereanylawstating"womenmust surrenderthemselvestothekingifitishiswish,regardlessoftheirmarital status.Inanycase,beingthehighestauthorityintheland,thekingsand rulerscouldgetawaywithalltheirflingswithnoquestionsasked.Ifanyone daredtoquestionthem,itwouldprobablyevenresultintheirdeath.From thewomen'sperspective,manyofthemwouldbewilling,marriedornot,to haveafling,sincebeingclosertothekingmeantbeingclosertowealthand power. There have been some cases in history where a marriage was arrangedbetweenamistressandsomemaninthecourtbecausetheking wanted to have an affair with her. A single woman might not have justificationforbeingaroundthepalaceallthetime,butthewifeofthis or that official would be expected to be there.

These were, of course, marriages of convenience, but it is interesting to see who were they convenientfor!

India has seen numerous Kings and Queens; these rulers battled in war, worked for the welfare of their kingdom, built big excellent castles, and managed many numerous different issues.

However, their private lives were very intriguing as well. While

carrying on their day-to-day affairs of running their kingdom, they also had secret affairs during their reign, however, there were also some eavesdroppers within the royal walls, who knew most of the secrets. Some of them, let their whispers of secrets travel across the nation and thanks to them, we now have the privileged insights into the lives of these ancient rulers, whose secrets would have otherwise remained unknown. Let us now go back in history and have a look at some of the most intriguing love stories of our past rulers.

CHAPTER ONE

JODHA AKBAR

"THE MYSTERIOUS RAJPUT PRINCESS EVERYONE KNOWS, BUT HAS NO EXISTENCE IN BOOKS"

Jodha Akbar is a sixteenth century love story about a marriage of alliance that gavebirth to true love between a great Mughal Emperor, Akbar, and a Rajput Princess, Jodha (her real name was Marium uz Zamani), who was the daughter of Raja Bharmal from Amber. Jodha was to be married to Raja Ratan Singh who would heritage the crown of her father after their marriage. Set in the sixteenth century, this epic romance begins as a marriage of alliance between two cultures and religions, for political gain, with the Hindu King Bharmal of Amber giving his daughter's hand to a Muslim Emperor, Akbar. When Akbar accepts the marriage proposal, little does he know that in his efforts to strengthen his relations with the Rajputs, he would in turn be embarking on a new journey---the journey of "true love." From the battlefield where the young Jalaluddin was crowned, through the conquests that won him the title of Akbar the Great, to winning the love of the beautiful Jodha, Jodha Akbar traces the impressive graph of themighty emperor and his romance with the defiant princess. It will be interesting to notethat there is little clarity on the total number of wives that Akbar eventually had.

History does not corroborate any instance of Akbar's romance with Jodhabai in the real sense. Yet there seems to be unanimity over Jodha bai being referred to as Akbar's favorite Queen. In fact, she was his third wife. What possibly could have been the reason for this? Jodha, it is said, was extremely gorgeous and dignified. But apart from her personality, she gave Akbar what his other Queens could not---an heir. Akbar's first queen was the childless Ruqaiyya Begum, and his second wife was Salima Sultan, the widow of his most trusted general, Bairam Khan.

It is said and observed that a sense of desperation seemed to mark Akbar's prayers at the dargah of the Shaikh Salim Chishti, which later led to the birth of his first surviving child, Jahangir. Did this result in Akbar becoming more closer and loving towards Jodhabai? Subsequently, it is said that Jodhabai enjoyed increased clout over political matters. She was the only Queen of Akbar who could issue farman (official decree), which was normally the exclusive privilege of the Emperor. This influence gave her the power to build gardens, wells, and mosques around the country. Jodhabai was allowed to practice Hinduism freely. She is said to have been politically involved in the court until Nur Jahan became Empress. According to Thomas Roe, she was involved in active sea trade and owned a ship named Rahimi which carried pilgrims to Mecca. In 1613, her ship, the Rahimi, was seized by the

Portugese pirates along with 700 passengers and the cargo. When the Portugese refused to return the ship and the passengers,there was a huge outcry at the Mughal Court. Jodha's son, the

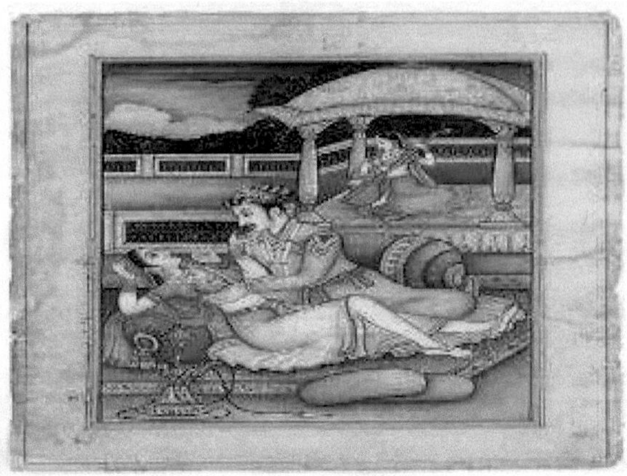

Indian Emperor, Jahangir, ordered the seizure of the Portuguese town Daman. This episode is considered to be an example of the struggle for wealth that would later ensure and lead to colonization of the Indian sub-continent.

It is also accepted that Jodha had the permission to worship in the Hindu way in her palace and she continued to remain a devotee of Lord Krishna. Akbar's fondness of Jodha, only made him more accepting of Hindu rituals. That Jahangir, Akbar's successor, too is appreciated as a liberal leader, perhaps only shows the indirect influence that Jodha might have made politically. Having dwelt upon Jodha's preferred status in Akbar's life, Akbar's subsequent marriages cannot be wished away, and this is where the soft romance between Akbar and Jodha gets mired in irony.

In all likelihood, Jodha, in the limited way that she could, gave Akbar a sense of belonging that his other women could not. In all probability, she reduced Akbar's personal detachment and made him discover a side of his that had got dwarfed by his political ambitions. She became one of the chief wives of Emperor Akbar after her marriage. Though she remained aHindu, Jodha Bai was honored with the title Mariam-uz-Zamani which means "Mary of the Age" after she gave birth to Jahangir. Despite her being a Hindu, she held great honor in theMughal household. Apart from the title of Mariam-uz-Zamani, Jodha also held the titles of Mallika-e-Muezzama, Mallika-e-Hindustan and Wali Nimat Begam which means the Gift of God. Jodha Bai was reported to have been a very smart business woman, who ran an active international trade in spices and silk.

She was one of the only four members of the court (another was the emperor)and the only woman to have the rank of 12,000 cavalry and was known to receive a jewel from every nobleman "according to his estate" each year on the o ccasion of New Year's festival. Like only a few other women at the Mughal Court, Mariam-uz-Zamani (Jodha

Bai) was granted the right to issue official documents (singularly called farman), usually the exclusive privilege of the Emperor. Issuing of such orders was confined to the highest ladies of the harem such as Hamida Banu Begum, Mariam-uz-Zamani, Nur Jehan, Mumtaz Mahal, Nadira Banu, and Jahanara Begum. Jodha Bai used her wealth and influence to build gardens, wells, and mosques around the countryside. Akbar allowed Jodha to perform the customary Hindu rites in the royal palace. He also let her maintain a Hindu temple in the palace. In fact, Akbar too sometimes participated in the puja she performed.

Ten days after his 63rd birthday, the greatest of the Great Moguls died of dysentery in his capital of Agra. At around midnight on 25 October, death took him. He was buried in the mausoleum he himself had built at Sikandra outside Agra. Mariam-uz-Zamani died in 1623. Even in her death, she remained closest to her husband. She is Akbar's only wife to be buried close to him, as per her wish. A *vav* or step well was constructed by her son, Emperor Jahangir, as per her last wishes. The grave itself is underground with a flight of stepsl eading to it. Her tomb, built in 1623- 27, is on the Tantpur road now known as Jyoti Nagar. Though she remained a Hindu throughout her life, she was buried according to Islamic tradition, near her husband's mausoleum. Her tomb is only a kilometer away from the Tomb

of Akbar the g reat the tomb's location reduced its chances of becoming a tourist attraction, but likewise, its lack of visibility meant it fell into a state of disrepair. Later, taken over by ASI, her resting place is now dignified.

TOMB OF EMPEROR AKBARLOCATED AT: - AGRA

TOMB OF MARIAM-LOCATED AT :- UZ- ZAMANI- SIKANDRA

"JODHA WAS KNOWN AS AKBAR'S FIRST AND LAST LOVE"
14

CHAPTER TWO

RAMA-SITA

"TRUST YOUR LOVE ENOUGH TO OVERCOME ANY CHALLENGE"

Rama and Sita are viewed as a perfect couple in mythology. Their love story is told and retold because as a woman, Sita is looked at as the person who preferred undergoing hardships of living in the forest rather than the palace as she chose to remain close to her husband. On his part, her husband also did notleave her side for a moment, took care of her as much as possible, but destiny had other plans.

To begin with, Rama is the masculine incarnate of divinity. He was the prince of a kingdom known as Kosala which was said to be the greatest kingdom on Earth. The charming epitome of the "perfect man," he had all the divine noble qualities that view Spirit as the Ultimate Reality. Rama is also a mantra that represents truebalance and harmony. He's also regarded as the model Yogi for Rama upholds truth (satya) and virtue in every right action he takes. Sita was a princess, and also a daughter of Mother Earth. destined for Rama. As such, she carried all the earthly values: fertility, transformation, deep patience, extraordinary beauty and yin-like passivity. Her love was the kind that surrendered to her divine destiny—a destiny that united her in this epic love story with Rama. Theirs is a supreme love-at-first-sight kind of story. Rama happened to come to a town where Sita lived and as soon as he rests his eyes upon the lovely Sita, her immediately falls deeply in love with her. They are soul mates in every sense of the term. Their attraction is divine,and they have somehow found each other in this material world.

The Ramayana has long been treated as something of a **moralcodebook**in Hindu society. Every action of Ram and Sita is treated as part of a godly plan, and the sweet imperfections of a man-woman relationship are forgotten. If you happen to come across a woman feminist and speak on this topic, be ready with some ready repugnance for Ram. After all, which self-respecting, free thinking woman would approve of a man who not only shames his wife but also abandons her during pregnancy? But this view is as reductive as the traditional one, which upholds Ram as the *maryadapurushottam*

Together, Rama and Sita incarnate as Vishnu and Lakshmi. Rama is the Vishnu incarnate, and Sita the Lakshmi one. Vishnu and Lakshmi are the protectors of the Universe and of the dharma (natural law). This means that the union of Rama and Sita is more than just any typical marriage. They are here to teach us what is right in terms of how the cosmos should function. They are here to model the dharma,

to be an example of how we should act and be.

Ram's character must be considered in its entirety; in most cases, he takes a morally hard stand, but he is almost pliant as a husband. Ram is an indulgent partner by any measure. Knowing fully well that the golden deer is an illusory rakshasa, he concedes to Sita's demands and agrees to fetch it for her. If he did not care for her, he would have refused. Ram's proof of love, unfortunately, becomes the morbid turning point of the tale and Sita is abducted by Ravana. With the aid of tricky monkey king, Hanuman, Rama rescues Sita, defeating Ravana and the evil rakshasas. In doing so, Rama rids the planet of all evil.

When Ram returns, he finds Sita has disappeared and is in great distress. He is disconsolate, shattered. In his haze of grief, he starts asking the animals and trees whether they have seen Sita and loses his will to live. It is only when Lakshman hammers some sense into the brain of his elder brother, that Ram begins to realize his folly and becomes a man with a mission.

The Ramayana also explores the romantic side of Ram-Sita's relationship. Sita narrates her story to Hanumana when he first goes to Lanka to get news of her. One day, on the Chitrakuta hill, when the couple is resting, a hungry crow attacks Sita. He pecks at her breasts a couple of times, distressing her greatly. Seeing his beloved in a distressed state, Ram, in a fit of rage, plucks a blade of kusha grass,breathes magic into it, turns it into

a brahmastra and unleashes it on the erring bird. Scared, the bird flies around the world trying desperately to avoid the arrow, but the divine arrow does not stop chasing it. In the end, it surrenders to Ram and seeks his protection.But a brahmastra once unleashed cannot be taken back and so the compassionate hero spares the crow's life and says that the weapon would strike him only in one eye.

Full credit must be given to Ram. In defense of his lady love, whether it may be a mere crow or the mighty King of Lanka, is something worth endearing. Ram actsas a lover and a dutiful husband. On the other hand, his eventual decisions pertaining to her agnipareeksha and banishment are made as a king. Ram's heartbreak is palpable even the second time around, torn as he is between his love for his wife and his duties as a king. Eventually as a king he must keep his subjects happy and so he chooses the harder option. But he never takes another wife and uses Sita's golden image during religious ceremonies, while being constantly scoffed at for his loyalty towards an apparently unworthy woman.

Sita's acquiescence to everything Ram does is not merely wifely obedience either. She is feisty in her own way and if she chooses silence or suffering, it is for the cause of love. She knows and values Ram's love too much to want to stay behind in Ayodhya or to give in to Ravana's threats and temptations, but she keeps her side of the marital pact as long as she lives.

Each character Rama and Sita encounter and the situations with each meeting teach us valuable life lessons. We learn the values of dharma and our duty to love, respect and take care of our loved ones. Both Rama and Sita uphold 'satya' at all costs. They are the perfect example of "right living" and we can learn from their words and actions whenever we immerse ourselves in the "Ramayana." The dramas that take place in the Ramayana reflect the passion and devotion between these two lovers and remain an inspiration to us to this day.

That the face of Ram's love changes disappointingly at the end of the journey,is another matter. But that love, brought them closer together, inspired them to walk the road together and this is what should be an inspiration to all of us.The love story of Ram and Sita has many layers; we just need to be perceptive to understand better.

In love. Always Rise in love, never say We fell in love, always say We feel the LOVE

CHAPTER THREE

SHIVA-PARVATI

"PURE LOVE IS A WILLINGNESS TO GIVE WITHOUT EXPECTING ANYTHING"

Parvati, often incarnated as Kali and Durga, was, in fact, a reincarnation of Sati (or Dakshayani), the daughter of the God Daksha. She practiced severe penance to win Lord Shiva's heart and after years of Tapasya at the Gauri Kund, Parvati succeeded in convincing Lord Shiva to accept her as his wife. Shiva was the God of the Yogis, self-controlled and celibate, while at the same time a remarkable love for his spouse. He is the destroyer, following Brahma the creator and Vishnu the preserver, after which Brahma again creates the world and so on. Shiva is responsible for change, both in the form of death and destruction and in the positive sense of destroying the ego, the false identification.

Many of us often suppress our highest potential and often hurt by our past experiences, we shield our emotional body to protect ourselves from further injury. This process of retreat is mimicked by Shiva when he lost his great beloved Sati. In grief, Shiva sat in meditation for thousands of years neglectinghis duties of dissolution and destruction. One day, Brahma, the God of creation, looked around and saw that nature was looking very dull and lost most of its beauty. It was like everything was stagnated. Brahma ran out of ideas and his imagination was blocked. So he went to the great feminine force, Shakti, for help. Shakti told Brahma that she would be born in a human female form to bring Shiva back into the world.

Shakti was reborn as Parvati. Her whole life, Parvati, had a special love in her heart for Shiva. As a young girl, she sat in the meadow fluttering her eyes at him, placing flowers at his feet, cooing his name, and daydreaming about him opening his eyes, taking her into his arms, and feeling love's embrace. Yet this never happened.

All her daydreaming was not doing anything but frustrating her. It was then that she decided to act. She went to the God of love, Kama, and asked him to shoot an arrow into Shiva's heart in order to arouse him as she was quite confident that this would achieve the desired result. Kama did accordingly and shot an arrow into Shiva's heart, enraging him and bringing him out of meditation. With a roar, he opened his third eye,and fire shot out which incinerated Kama. Shiva then closed all his three eyes and retreated inward leaving Parvati frustrated as her plan had failed.

Parvati then began to meditate. For thousands of years, she stood on one leg on hot coals and for thousands of years on the other leg in the cold snow. During her meditations, she builds tapas, inner heat, and her own power grows so strong that Shiva, deep in his meditation, feels her presence and awakens from his meditation. Shiva and Parvati then get married and in between their love making, discuss the science of yoga. Parvati did not gain S hiva's attention because she was beautiful. She was able to gain his attention because her inner light was brilliant. Although she encountered many twists and turns, she never gave up and proved that hard work and inner discipline are necessary for growth.

The wedding between Shiva the Adiyogi and Parvati was a grand affair. Since Parvati was a princess, the "who's who" of the region were invited; kings and queens, gods, and goddesses, each in their finery, one more beautiful than the other. When Shiva first appeared for the wedding, he was wearing the fresh skin of an elephant, dripping with blood and was looking all demented and distorted along with his entourage. Parvati's mother fainted on looking at him and the others also felt disgusted, but Parvati told Shiva that she did not mind the way he was as he was all that she wanted. She then requested him to change into something pleasant for the sake of her mother to which he readily agreed.

When he transformed himself and came to the wedding again, they said he was a '**Sundaramurti'** which means he was the most beautiful human being ever seen. He was approximately nine feet tall and when he stood, he was in level with the horse's head, and everyone was awestruck by his presence. For the bride, Parvati's father was the King of the Himalayan Mountain region. Many glorious things were said about the bride's lineage but when it came to the groom, nothing was said. This angered Humayun who was reluctant to hand over his daughter to a man who had no lineage, but then his sage Narada said that the groom had no father or mother, and he was born out of reverberation and had no parentage, no antecedents, and no lineage. he was "Swayambhu" self – created, a being without antecedents. The king got freaked out but eventually the wedding did take place.

When their son Kartikeya was born, he was given to the Kritikas because Shiva believed that this would imbibe skills that would help in warfare later. After coming to Kailasha, he immediately went to train to fight **Tarakasura**, one of the strongest demons in Hindu mythology. Shortly after killing him, he was sent to another kingdom for his protection. So, Parvati wasn't given much opportunity to enjoy the company of her son and she was motivated to go for meditation.

Shiva and Parvati always supported each other through thick and thin. Right from preparing bhang to making quilts, they would do it all together. They also argued-like every other couple- only to reconcile later and grow fonder of each other as we can observe from their following conversations:

Parvati: It is my great privilege that, because of my actions in my previous births, you have become my husband and I your wife.

Shiva: I will always protect you with my love. You remain without concern. I will remainwith you both in pleasure and in pain.

Parvati: In circumstances of pain, I will maintain patience, and in pleasure, I will express my delight. In both pleasure and in pain, I will always be with you. I will protect and nourish our children, my husband, and our family.

Shiva: I will provide all the necessities for life for our family, including food, clothing, and shelter, whatever is needed. I will seek your agreement inall matters of household life.

Parvati: I will remain contented in any standard you choose to maintain us, and I will always respect and obey your every order. I will always prepare food for you and our family and assure you that you will always be satisfied with my food.

Shiva: I will always enjoy whatever you give me to eat, and I will never have desires from any other woman. I will not make any other woman my source of nourishment.

Parvati: I will always adorn myself appropriately, and I will act appropriately in every circumstance. I will dedicate my mind, body, and soul to your satisfaction.

Shiva: Without you, I will not perform any actions of Dharma, Yajna, or Puja, or even pursue material gain. You will always be present as the motivation from my every action.

Parvati: In Puja, Yajna, and all acts of Dharma, I will always be present to help you. Without you, I will not contemplate anyone else's puja, yajna, or acts of dharma.

Shiva: I will always dedicate my mind and renunciation of all selfishness to your greatest delight.

Parvati: Wherever you stay, there will I also stay; wherever you dwell, I will also dwell by your side. I will never become tired from my beloved or from our love.

Shiva: I will never question your authority to be by my side. I will never leave you or renounce your love. I live with the hope that you will be my source of comfort eternally.

Parvati: All present here are witnesses that you are my husband and my Lord, and I have offered myself to you completely and eternally.

Shiva: I will always give you, my respect. Your desires will be the most important goals of my life. I will never consider that you are inferior to me. You will always be with me as my partner, as I with you.

"The affection that Lord Shiva and Goddess Parvati shared for each other is well-known!"

CHAPTER FOUR

SHAJAHAN-MUMTAZ SHAJAHAN-MUMTAZ MAHAL

"I FOUND THE TAJ MAHAL MOST APPROPRIATE EXAMPLE OF ARTISTICALLY EXPRESSED LOVE"

he love of the great Moghul Emperor, Shah Jahan, for his wife

With stands court intrigue, dynastic betrayal, war, and death itself when he builds her the greatest memorial tomb of all time: the TAJ MAHAL. The Taj Mahal, chosen as one of the 'Seven Wonders of the New World,'is the fruit of a legendary love story. Countless people from all over the world visit this unique work built by Muslim Turks in India, but most are unaware of its history. The Mughal rulers demonstrated a trait that is not known to everyone and, in fact, unexpected given their strong military identities. This feature is their incomparable devotion to their wives.

The **TajMahal**is a mausoleum built by the Mughal Emperor Shah Jahan, also known as Hurram Shah Jahan, for his beloved wife Mumtaz Mahal,or Arjumand Banu-Begum Mumtaz

Mahal, in the city of Agra. It is the biggest and most beautiful monument erected in the name o f "LOVE" in the world.

Once upon a time, the nobles used to sell their handicrafts at a charity sale called Mina Bazaar and do good deeds with the money collected. Shah Jahan, who was a prince at that time, met his maternal relative, 20-year-old Mumtaz Mahal, here. He was fascinated by her beauty and intelligence. It was here that one of the greatest loves in history was born. He was only 14 years old, but the prince immediately told his father he wanted to marry the beautiful young princess. As was common, the Emperor Jahangir arranged the betrothal of the exquisite Arjumand Banu Begum to his son, Prince Khurram---they were to be married in five years' time.

In 1612, the astrologers of the palace selected the date May 10th for the young couple to be married---a day which, according to the stars, would be most beneficial to a long and happy marriage. Arjumand Banu Begum was unquestionably the love of the prince's life and so, in honor of his love and in tribute to her incontestable beauty, he bestowed on her the name Mumtaz Mahal, loosely translating to Jewel of the Palace. One could only imagine the life this wildly romantic couple would have experienced, midnight strolls on the shores of the Taj Lake, mid summer's night picnics in the Moonlight Garden of the palace---perhaps even an elephant ride for two through the streets of Agra or along the banks of the Yamuna River.

Following the prince's ascension to the Peacock Throne, he came to be known as the Mughal Emperor Shah Jahan and throughout his reign, Mumtaz Mahal was loyally by his side. She was his trusted companion and undisputed soul mate, and despite her frequent pregnancies would, without fail, travel throughout the Mughal

Empire with her husband on his various military campaigns and royal visits. Shah Jahan loved and trusted Mumtaz Mahal so much, that he even presented her with the greatest h onor possible — his imperial seal, the Muhr Uzah.

In 1631, while accompanying her husband on a campaign to the Deccan Plateau, Mumtaz Mahal gave birth to her fourteenth child, a daughter, but resulted in a very tragic ending which was her death during labor. As Mumtaz Mahal took her last breaths, Shah Jahan vowed to her that he would never remarry, and would build her the most magnificent mausoleum as her tomb. Following his wife's death, the emperor was inconsolable — he ordered the country into two years of mourning, and he himself went into solitude.

Eventually, the Emperor's eldest daughter, the devoted Jahanara Begum, helped him to arise from his twelve long months of solitude, but by then, his hair had turned white, his back was bent, and his face worn. However, Shah Jahan intended to keep the promise he made to his beloved wife and began work on erecting the most extraordinary sepulcher in the world. The monument took 22 years and the labor of over 22,000 men, and once completed, it looked magnificent.

A SHINING MONUMENT OF ONE OF THE GREATEST LOVE STORIES OF HISTORY!

CHAPTER FIVE

BAJIRAO-MASTANI

"ONLY IF THE MEETING IS INCOMPLETE, THEN THE PROMISE TO MEET AGAIN, IS MADE"

In the 18th century, men could take several wives and mistresses in the name of polygamy. They could openly cheat their legit wives with multiple spouses and mistresses. Women were very much subdued and had to keep their mouths shut since they had no financial backing and social freedom could not separate. Hence, they had to keep quiet and tolerate the presence of concubines. Peshwa Bajirao the first, a descendent of prime ministers who served Pune's rulers including Shivaji, later succeeded him as ruler of the region. He fought 41 battles for the King Chhatrapati Sahuji Maharaja, and never lost one which earned him great respect across the Maratha Kingdom. Mastani was given to him in marriage by her father Raja Chattrasal of Bundelkhand, after the Peshwas helped him when the enemies attacked his small kingdom. Mastani was a beautiful woman, and talented-

--she was brought up like a Kshatriya Princess with mastery in horse riding, sword fighting, religious studies etc. She was also an accomplished singer and dancer whose translucent skin was likened to the finest pearl and her mouth to the red pomegranate seed which completely captivated Bajirao.

Brahmins were monogamous. Bajirao Peshwa was a Brahmin and already married. Mastani, being of Muslim faith, could not become his legit wife and so she stuck to being treated as his favorite companion and mistress for a period spanning a decade. The wife of Bajirao, Kashibai, accepted the relationship between Bajirao and Mastani; whether she was forced to do so, or she mutually accepted their relationship is unknown. In any case, she did not have much choice. Peshwa beingthe most powerful authority at that time, did not care for any opposition and made a separate Mastani darwaza in Shaniwar Wada, where Mastani moved in.

Mastani was given the best attention whereas Kashibai suffered in silence. Peshwas even wanted to elevate her status to that of his wife after she gave birth to a son. Although he maintained a relationship with both Kashibai and Mastani for some years, his attention was more focused on Mastani and he started spending more time with her. Kashibai felt ignored and lonely. Although the relationship of Peshwa and Mastani was celebrated by some people as good for a Hindu-Muslim alliance, there was staunch opposition from the Brahmin society. An undeterred Peshwa, unheeding the advice of his mother and brother, nurtured al illicit relationship, as if he had the free license to exploit his power.

R egardless of what others had to say, Bajirao, had a beautiful palace built for his b eloved, in which terracotta painted walls, embellished with themes from the K irshna Leela, were drawn with the finest strokes, in white. The wooden ceiling was in tricately carved and supported on equally ornate carved pillars. Wonderful crystal ch andeliers lit up the palace, and as the Peshwa dressed in his fine silks, relaxed a gainst gold embroidered velvet cushions, his beloved Mastani played on the ta npura, lifting her melodious voice in song. These two did not need anything more to make their happiness complete.

In their hands, Mastani grew out of being one of history's many ciphers into a brave woman passionately devoted to her husband, an accomplished horse rider who accompanied her husband into battle and someone who fought tooth and nail t o protect their son from forces who were out to kill them.

Unfortunately, their romance was doomed from the start and moved to its sad and not natural end. In Bajirao's ill-fated love affair with his Muslim wife Mastani, religion played a major part in their problems. As it happens with many love stories, the fact that Bajirao's second wife was half-Muslim didn't augur well with his family. The situation became worse with Bajirao showering all his love and affection towards Mastani, neglecting his first wife Kashibai in the process. A feeling of anger and jealousy crept in within the family members towards Mastani who by this week time was actively participating in state affairs. Mastani was never accepted as one of their own by Bajirao's brother, Chimaji Ballal Peshwa and mother Radhabai. He tried to send her into exile. While the Peshwa was away on a military campaign, his son Balaji placed Mastani under house arrest. Realizing the hatred of his family, Bajirao built "Mastani Mahal" in north-east corner of his palace at Shaniwar Wada in Pune. The building had its external doorway.

The death of Bajirao is still shrouded in mystery. Some say he died from heatstroke while inspecting his estate near the city of Indore. Others say he died in battle and there are still others who say that Bajirao died because of Alcohol withdrawal. It is said that he made a vow to his mother to give up alcohol in lieu of Mastani being accepted in the family and sent to him. But the emotional trauma of the news of Mastani's death aggravated with his physical suffering proved fatal for him. It is said that Mastani couldn't bear the tragedy and died soon afterwards by drinking poison. Whatever may be the truth, but Bajirao's love for Mastani was real and perpetual. The reconstructed part of the Mastani Mahal lives on in the Museum, as a tribute to the grandeur of a by gone era and a reminder of one of the great r omances of our land.

LOCATED AT :- A DISTANCE OF 60 KMS FROM PUNE IN THE VILLAGE PABAL, THE GRAVE OF MASTANI IS LOCATED IN THE MIDDLE OF A 2,000 SQ FT LAND.

CHAPTER SIX

MAHARAJA RANJIT SINGH AND MORAN SARKAR

NOT ONLY A GREAT WARRIOR, BUT ALSO, A BRILLIANT ADMINISTRATOR

As the legend is told, it so happened that the young Maharaja Ranjit Singh, happened to see this girl, originally said to be from Kashmir, performing a dance in the Royal Baradari (pavilion) in Dhanoa Kalan village. As she danced, her graceful and fluent movements impressed him to such an extent, that he fell madly in love with her and thus gave her the title 'Moran,' which means 'peacock.' He immediately decided to marry her creating an uproar! When you think of the powerful image of the one-eyed warrior and empire builder, Maharaja Ranjit Singh of Punjab, it is hard to imagine that as a 22-year-old, he was prepared to accept social outrage onthe command of the Akhal Takht, for wanting to marry a Muslim *nautch*girl.

According to another local legend, one day, when Moran was going to Baradari for her dance performance, her anklet/shoe fell into a canal while she was crossing. This enraged her to such a great extent that she refused to perform until a bridge (Pul Kanjari) was built over the canal. A besotted Ranjit Singh quickly had a bridge built at the site and it stands here to this day. It is called 'Pul Moran.' **TheyoungRanjitSinghwassomuchinlovewithMoran, thatheproposedmarriagetoherandagreedtoalltheconditionsshehad laiddowntobehiswife,themainonebeingthathetakepermission fromherfather.Thelove-struckRanjitSinghcompliedhumbly.**

They both got married amidst great fanfare in 1802.The processions began at Lahore's Shalimar Bagh. A wealthy businessman, Samad Joo Kashmiri, a renowned noble acted as Moran's father during the ceremonies. and even took care of the bridal expenses. The marriage was said to have taken place in his haveli in Amritsar. After the wedding, the couple went to Hardwar for a dip in the holy Ganga. They then went to Lahore and Moran was given her own beautiful Haveli or villa, specially constructed by the Maharaja for her in the Papar Mandi area inside Lahore's Shah Alami gate.

After pain staking research, Manveen Sandhu, Principal of Springdale Senior School, Amritsar, established that Maharaja Ranjit Singh had married the Muslim dancer as part of his social reform movement and to win over the other communities. Research of Ms Sandhu also revealed that Moran was not a *nautch* girl but belonged to a family of entertainers. Moran's charm captivated the Maharaja's heart when he was just 21. His was a transition from physical to spiritual love and attachment. The Maharaja soon realized the women in Moran's community were being exploited by society. To give a message to society at large, he decided to sanctify his love for her by marrying her. He made an effort to uplift Moran's community. Moran's **'biradari'** lived in a village called Makhanwindi near Amritsar. The Maharaj gave the biradari a place near Amritsar city and named it Sharifpura to rehabilitatehonor of the community and encourage them to explore other vocations in case they wished to do so. She led a life of simplicity and piety after marriage with the Maharaja.

According to historical chroniclers, Moran was a very competent and able administrator. She went about setting up her own court in the haveli, from where she could listen to the grievances of the people. She was a close confidant and advisor to the Maharaja and was soon given the title of "**Moran Sarkar**" by the locals. She also requested the Maharaja to construct a mosque close by to her haveli (Jamia Masjid Tarro Moran), which he duly obliged. Tarro is a Persian phrase meaning 'revolving.' Moran's dance career of her early years was mentioned to be famous for fast round revolutions. Thus, she earned the name.

There are many accounts which paint Moran as a popular "**People's Queen**." She has also been credited with the building of the Shivala Temple in the Lahore Fort and, a madrasa, in 1823. The esteem that Moran enjoyed during her time, is evident from the fact that between 1802 and 1827, a series of coins was introduced by the Sikh Empire's mint, known as "**Moran Shahi.**" These coins had a peacock's feather inscribed on them and were symbolic of her.

Moran had met Ranjit Singh when he had a small kingdom not stretching more than a few miles from the capital city of Lahore. But she died very young and was not able to see her husband become the empire builder that history knows him tobe. There are also no records of the date or the cause of her death, except that it was a 'natural' one.

Moran is today regarded as Mai (Mother) Moran in Pakistan and the mosque she constructed in Papar Mandi in Lahore is named after her. The residents there believed she was a great lady who did a lot of good for her people. In contrast, in the Indian side of the Punjab, she is described in disrespectful terms such as '**Kanjri**' and '**Tawaif**' due to the stigma of being *anautch*girl before her marriage. Similarly, the bridge being built by Maharaja Ranjit Singh according to Moran's wishes also came to be known as "Pul Kanjri" by the locals after the fall of the Sikh Empire.

MORAN MOSQUE**LOCATED AT :- PAPAR MANDI-LAHORE**

PUL KANJARILOCATED AT :- ON THE WAGAH BORDER

The chroniclers of Ranjit Singh, like diplomat and historian Fakir Syed Waheeduddin in his book, "The Real Ranjit Singh" mention how heartbroken the Maharaja was when he lost Moran and how often he remembered her.

CHAPTER SEVEN

SALIM - ANARKALI

FOR SALIM, IT WAS LOVE AT FIRST SIGHT AND SOON ANARKALI TOO FELL IN LOVE WITH THE CHARMINGPRINCE"

The original name of Anarkali was Nadira Begum or Sharf-un-Nisa

but this legendary courtesan was given the nickname 'Anarkali' as she became the central focal point of love interest of the Mughal Prince Salim, who later became the Emperor Jahangir.

In his childhood days, Salim was very mischievous and stubborn and his father Emperor Akbar, sent him to a distant military school to overcome his stubbornness. Having completed his education and training, Salim returned home after a period of 14y ears, which made Akbar happy and so he organized a big 'mujra' (ceremony) in his palace. To increase the charm of the ceremony, Akbar invited his favorite dancer Nadira, whose real name was "Sharif Un Nissa". She was so beautiful in appearance and graceful in her dance, that people gave her the name 'Anarkali,' which means "beauty bud."

As the legend is told, and the saying goes "Love at first sight," it was at this ceremony Salim, son of Emperor Akbar, set his eyes on Anarkali, and he immediately fell in love with this beautiful courtesan lady. The title 'Anarkali' signifies "pomegranate blossom"

(a title bestowed for her beauty). Besides being a beautiful lady, she was also famed for her dancing skills. This mesmerized Prince Salim, who fell in love as soon as he saw her. But for a royal family, a dancing girl is just a dancing girl, and they did not consider her of noble birth. She was considered as being low-born and keeping any relation with the low born people was considered strictly taboo by the society. Moreover, she was not just a dancer, she was also the main prostitute of t hat city.

Anarkali was aware of this fact and knew that her romance with Prince Salim was strictly objected by Salim's father, Emperor Akbar, and if he came to know about their love affair, he would have her killed. So, she tried her best to keep away from S alim, but the problem was for how long could she sustain this? As it is said, "Love has no rules" and so soon enough, Anarkali too fell deeply in love with Salim. But when Royalty steps in, there is bound to be trouble, and this came in the form of Emperor Akbar who highly objected to his son being in love with an ordinary courtesan. He could not digest the fact that his son Salim had fallen in love with a prostitute, with whom he too had a physical relationship. So, he started creating all sorts of tactics and pressurized her a lot in order to make her downfall in the eyes o f Salim, who was by this time, fully smitten with her love.

When Salim came to know about his father's Akbar's tactics, he could not digest this and in a fit of rage, he declared war against his own father. But the mighty army of Akbar proved too strong for the small army of Prince Salim, who was defeated and sentenced to death. The love of Anarkali for Salim was so much that she renounced her love to save her beloved from the jaws of death. She went to Akbar and pleaded with him to leave Salim without killing him. Akbar then replied, 'If you are ready to be away from Salim forever, I will forgive him." She was entombed in a brick wall right in front of her lover's eyes. It is said, however, that she did not die as the tomb was constructed on the opening of a secret tunnel unknown to Salim. It is said that she escaped through that tunnel and fled the place, never to return. The heart broken Salim lived on to become Emperor Jahangir.

Salim became a fractal lover after being away from Anarkali. After the death of Emperor Akbar, he became the Mughal Emperor with a new name Jahangir. While he was dying, Anarkali's name was on his lips.

CHAPTER EIGHT

SHIVAJI-SAIBAI

"SAI WAS THE LAST WORD HE UTTERED ON HISDEATHBED. TRUE LOVENEVER ENDS"

Sai Bhosale (nee Sai Nimbalkar 1633-5 September 1659, was the first wife and chief consort of Chhatrapati Shivaji Maharaj, the founder of the Maratha Empire. S he was the mother of her husband's successor and the second Chhatrapati, Sambhaji. Saibai was a member of the prominent Nimbalkar family, whose members were the rulers of Phaltan from the era of the Yadava dynasty and served the Deccan Sultanates and the Mughal Empire. Although Saibai's father was the ruler of Phaltan, it was not always the case. He was held by Adil Shah's army and was kept in prison. Shahaji, Shivaji's father, helped him to escape and as an act of appreciation, Mudhojirao came up with a marriage proposal. This is how S hivaji, and Sai met and got married young in 1640.

It was a childhood marriage that took place between Saibai and Shivaji on 16 May, 1640 at Lal Mahal, Pune. The marriage was arranged by Shivaji's mother, Jijabai, but was evidently not attended by Shivaji's father, Shahaji nor his brothers, Sambhaji and Ekoji. Thus, Shahaji soon summoned his new daughter-in-law, Shivaji and his mother, Jijabai, to Bengaluru, where he lived with his second wife,Tukabai.

There was a very close relationship and a strong bond between Shivaji and Saibai. It is said that she was a wise woman and a loyal consort to Shivaji. Moreover, she was also very beautiful and charming, besides being a good-natured and affectionate woman. She is also described as having been a "gentle and selfless person."

Enter Caption

There is no record of any friction or mutual differences between her and Shivaji's other wives. If Saibai was alive, she was an asset to Shivaji, not only regarding the affairs of the State, but also regarding household affairs. She also had a significant influence over

her husband and the Royal family as well. During her lifetime, the entire household of Shivaji bore a homogenous atmosphere, even though most of her husband's marriages were performed due to political considerations.

During the course of their nineteen years of a peaceful and trouble-free married life, Saibai and Shivaji became parents of four children: Sakhubai, Ranubai, Amanika or Ambikabai and Sambhaji. The birth of Sambaji was an occasion of great joy and significance in the Royal household for many different reasons.

Saibai died in 1659 (aged 26) at Raigad while Shivaji was making preparations for his meeting with Afzal Khan at Pratapgad. She was ill from the time she gave birth to Sambhaji and her illness took a serious turn preceding her death. Sambhaji was two years old at the time of his mother's death and was brought up by his paternal grandmother,Jijabai, which entailed long spells of separation between Shivaji and his much-loved son Sambhaji. Saibai's Samadhi (Memorial) is situated at Raigad Fort.

After Saibai's untimely death in 1659 followed by Jijabai's death in 1674, Shivaji's private life became clouded with anxiety and unhappiness. Although his next wife, Soyarabai had gained prominence in the Royal Household following their deaths, she was not an affectionate consort like Saibai, whom Shivaji had dearly loved.

Although Shivaji had many wives (around 8), his best relationship was with his wife Saibai. They shared a life together and then when she left him for 20 years, he never forgot her, and no one could take the place of Saibai in his heart. She was his one true love... and then, of course, uttering her name 20 years later on his death bed proved that love does not need you to be physically present but even your essence being with your love is everything to them!

SAIBAI'S MEMORIAL

SHIVAJI'S MEMORIALLOCATED AT :- RAIGAD FORT

Saibai remained the favorite of Shivaji till he died. A great source of inspiration to him, legend has it that "Sai" was the last word he uttered on his deathbed.

TRUE LOVE NEVER ENDS!!!

CHAPTER NINE

QULI QUTUB SHAH AND BHAGMATI

"LOVE CONQUERS ALL, LET US ALL YIELD TO LOVE"

For some strange reason, all or almost all, love legends have a

tragic ending. Not many end with the happy ending "and they lived happily ever after." This is probably due to the lovers being separated by the cruel hands of society, scheming relatives, jealous rivals, misunderstandings etc., the list is endless. Behind this backdrop of tears and tragedies, swords and daggers, deceit and chicanery, there is a story of love which makes you believe that love can't be all that bad. This is one of those stories.

The fifth King of a dynasty that lasted over 170 years, comes to the throne is a t a very young age. He also falls in love at a very young age but what is not clear is that whether he fell in love before becoming the king or whether he became king first. In any case, both happened when he was in his teens. If he fell in love before becoming the king, he must have had an extremely open minded and levelheaded father, but as the story goes, it appears that he fell in love first which goes to prove that he had a liberal and tolerant father. It is said that "**Trueloveneverg rows old.**" So was the legend of Bhagmati. Hers was love made up of stolen moments---bitter, sweet, and poignant. **Shewasthedamselindistress and he the knight inshining armor.**

It is said that once when the prince was passing through a village, not far from the capital, he came across a very beautiful woman and fell head over heels in love with her. On her part, the woman also observed his love for her and reciprocated the sentiments. Soon, they began to meet regularly though surreptitiously.

FORT OF THE QUTUB SHAHI KINGS.

Nothing could stop the star-crossed lovers, not even the turbulent River Musi. On one occasion, to meet his love, the prince had to risk his life while crossing the river. The river was in space and seemed intent on drowning the village of his beloved; the prince urged his horse to jump into the raging torrent, somehow made it to the other shore and succeeded in rescuing her. The king got worried byseeing these infantile displays of bravado, but being a kind, liberal and large- hearted man, he understood that it would not be possible to stop his son from crossing the river and so he called for a bridge to be built across the river. Accordingly, the Puranapul bridge was built to facilitate crossing.

The prince came to the throne after the death of his father in 1580 and ruled till 1611. The name of the prince was Mohamad Quli Qutub Shah, and the name of his beloved was Bhagmati. Shortly after becoming king, he married his lady love and built a new capital city that he named after his beloved, now his queen. The city he named after her was known as Bhaganagar but was later renamed Hyderabad, once Bhagmati got converted to Islam, she was given the title Hyder Mahal.

Hyderabad was a beautiful city with palaces, gardens, religious and secular buildings and well laid out roads, the center piece of the city was **Charminar**. Almost a decade after their marriage, a daughter was born to the royal couple. The daughter was later married to a nephew of the king and eventually became queen when her husband succeeded his uncle to the throne.

CHARMINAR-HYDERABAD

This is the story that has been popular among the people of Hyderabad, the story of two lovers who did not care about religious orthodoxy, about court intrigues, about the ill t hat people spoke about women who danced and sang.

"Omnia vincit amor et nos cedamus amori"

"Love conquers all, let us all yield to love!

CHAPTER TEN

BIMBISARA AND AMRAPALI

"AN ENCHANTING SAGA BURIED WITHIN THE SANDS OF TIME"

Bimbisara (544-419 BCE) was a famous Indian King of the

Maghada Kingdom in ancient India. He was a pious and well administered king. His capital was Rajgriha which later changed to Pataliputra. He maintained cordial relations with neighboring kingdoms and Indian kings, among them Suddodhana, father of Buddha was one. First, in the history, he maintained the Marital alliances to expand his kingdom.

Amrapali was a great character in Indian history. She was the ethereal beauty of Vaishali, was known as a dancer and also a philosophical thoughts oriented woman.. Amrapali was founded at the foot of a mango tree in Vaishali but was unknown about the details of her was the capital city of Lichhavi republic. She was found at the trunk of the mango tree known as Ambapali and Amba which means mango tree. She was a beautiful courtesan in Vaishali and had the rich and famous vying for her attention. **ShewasincompleteaweofBuddha.**

King Manudev, the undisputed King of Vaishali happened to see her dance performance and immediately decided to own her. But he was upset when he heard of her childhood love for Pushpakumar and their soon to be marriage. He murdered Pushpakumar on the day of the marriage and made an official announcement declaring

Amrapali “**the brideofVaishali’**i.e the Nagarvadhu only to satisfy his mounting sexual urge. Amrapali was made Nagarvadhu and Vaishali Janpad Kalayani. (Janpath Kalyani was the term given to the most beautiful and talented

AMRAPALLI-

THE COURT DANCER

Stories of her beauty and talent travelled to the ears of Bimbisara, King of the hostile neighboring kingdom of Magadha. He attacked Vaishali and took refuge in Amrapali’s house. Bimbi Sara was a good musician and would often sing to her, and before long both Amrapali and Bimbisara fell in love with each other.Bimbisara was purely in love with Amrapali that he would go to any extent to make her feel happy.

Their romance and love was blooming every day and Amrapali was also so enchanted by the King’s charm and intelligence, that she loved him with all her emotions and passion. King Bimbisara then asked her to marry him, but when she heard of his true identity, she got angry and declined him. She then asked him to leave and cease his war. Bimbisara was so much in love with her that hedid as she had asked him, but this incident made him a coward in the eyes of the people of Vaishali. Amrapali bore him a son named Vimala Kondanna. Both couldn’t be together, and they became the disciples of Buddha in the later stage of their lives.

Bimbisara was brutally murdered by his own son, Ajatashatru as his son was tired of waiting to ascend the throne. Amrapali was so ashamed of her past life that she begged Buddha to change her life in the way of attaining salvation of life. Due to her request, Buddha blessed and accepted her as his disciple. From then on, she became Buddhist bhikkhus and gifted the mango

CHAPTER ELEVEN

Raja Man Singh Tomar and Mrignayani

**"HE GAVE GREAT IMPORTANCE
TO MUSIC AND ARTS AND IS CREDITED
FOR DEVELOPING THE ART OF DANCE"**

Traveling around Madhya Pradesh, every state-run handicraft emporium shop that you come across is named as Mrignayani. A beautiful lady with emphasis on her eyes can be seen painted on the walls. Mrignayani, meaning the lady with eyes like that of a deer. Having heard about her name many times by now, let us look at the story behind the lady with beautiful eyes.

Tales of love, hatred, passion, and courage echo through Gwalior Fort. While Man Mandir Palace reverberates tragic stories; Gujari Mahal echoes the harmony of love.

RajaManSinghTomaris memorialized eminently for the peace and glory he brought to Gwalior and for his love for **Mrignayani**, his ninth wife. His love story becomes a legendary tale. This is the love story of Raja Man Singh Tomar, the most revered king of Gwalior and his ninth wife Mrignayani.

Raja Mansingh's relationship with Mrignayani was special. Not only was he smitten by her beauty, but he also shared her passion for music. Consumed by his devotion to the love of his life, he built the **GujariMahal**.

He even dedicated a classical raga to his beautiful Gujar wife which he called **GujariTodi.** Mrignayani learned music from **Haridas**, the celebrated musician in Man Singh's court. Raja Man Singh and Mrignayani would enjoy music performances together in an underground music hall in Gujari Mahal.

When Raja Man Singh went on a hunting expedition, he comes across a Gujar girl. Her name was **Ninni.** Some say she was hunting a buffalo while others say she was rescuing two buffaloes by untangling their tangled horns. You might have heard stories of how men tame the buffaloes to impress and marry girls, here the story is t he other way round. The Gujar girl was seen handling two buffaloes which were fighting and got their horns tangled. She is seen untangling the horns of two mighty buffaloes and the king is super carried away with her beauty, bravery, and valour.

Completely impressed by the blend of beauty, strength, and courage; the king right away to fell in love with her and asked her to be his queen. The beautiful and headstrong Gujar girl agreed on her own terms. She put forth three conditions:

1. **Equal status (nopardah)**
2. **PermissiontoaccompanyRajaeveninthebattleground.**She will accompany the king wherever he goes, that would be for hunting or to the court or to the battlefield. From the Gwalior Fort there is a separate path that leads to the Gujari Mahal. So, every time he comes back to the fort or leaves the fort he uses this path, stops by the Mahal, and then proceeds.
3. **SeparatepalacewiththeincessantsupplyofwatersofriverRaifromhervillage. Shebelievedthatitwaswaterfromthatriverthathadmadeherstrongandbeautiful.**

The smitten Man Singh does that too. That is also one of the reasons cited to having the palace at a lower level and not inside the fort up the hill as it was difficult to construct ducts that could push the water up hill.

The king agreed and married Ninni. He named her Mrignayani – the gazelle- eyed one. The enamoured Raja Man Singh built an aqueduct to bring water from the river to Gwalior. It was difficult to get water to travel uphill.

He built her a separate palace at the foot of Fort hillock. Gujari Mahal is within the Gwalior Fort premises a little away from the main palace.

Legends say the reason behind the separate palace was Mrignayani's wish to live in a palace built just for her with 24 hours water supply from the river Rai. Locals say that Mrignayani's palace was built away from the main palace because of her lower caste status.

Sadly, their story was short-lived. Like all love stories, this story too ended in a tragedy. Man, Singh's eight queens did not accept Mrignayani, and their fathers felt disgraced for their son-in-law had married a girl of a lower caste. They pulled back their aid. Islamic invaders (Mughals) attacked the fort; Man, Singh and his beautiful wife were killed in the battle owing to a lack of proper support and armies. Unwilling to submit to the invader, the other eight queens jumped into the p its of fire and ended their lives.

Rani Mrignayani and Raja Man Singh Tomar lived in love with each other until the invaders attacked and took over Gwalior. It is a till death do us apart story.

Gujari Mahal is located at the eastern gate of the fort called Gwalior Gate or Quila Gate. The narrow and dirty lanes took us to a huge gate. The palace gate and the passage that leads to the Gujari Mahal were thronged with locals.

Gujjari Mahal

A huge gate with two guardian lions on either side welcomes visitors. It's a treasure trove of ancient heritage and exquisite sculptures collected from various places, some dating back to the 1st and 2nd centuries BCE. The place literally stuns you.

Today, the Gujjari Mahal is an Archaeological Museum managed by the **Directorateof Archeology,Archives,andMuseums,MadhyaPradesh.** It's also called the **State ArcheologicalMuseum**or **GwaliorFortMuseum.**

The palace was converted into an archaeological museum in 1920 and was opened to the public in 1922. It houses around 28 galleries with almost 9000 antique pieces

The architecture of the stone monument is just breath taking. Built in the 15th century i n a traditional Hindu style architecture, the square palace has an open area in the center. The Persian inscription at the entrance narrates the story of

the making of the Gujjari M ahal.

Historical Treasures at Gujjari Mahal Archeological Museum

The museum collection includes- vintage coins, devotional statues, inscriptions, art pottery, weapons, jewels, bronze antiques, etc. Some of the rare collections of stone carvings and artwork will spellbind you.

The collection of vintage coins is mind-boggling. The museum puts on show the vast variety of gold, copper, alloy, and silver coins dating back to as early as 300B C.

Sculptures from **Suhania**, **Mitawali**, and **tree Goddess** are worth seeing. The depiction of the birth of Lord Krishna is beautiful.

Among the most striking artifacts are a large, late 9th to the early 10th-century sculpture of the **ShalbhanjikaYakshi**from Gyraspur (Indian Mona Lisa) and figures of **Nataraja Ardhanareshwar** and **Yama**.

"GLIMPSE OF GUJARI MAHAL, GWALIOR"

How to Reach Gujari Mahal, Gwalior:

Gwalior has an airport. Connected well through Railways and bus as well. It is in the town as opposed to the Gwalior fort.

Today Gujari Mahal is an archaeological museum. wading through the narrow streets of Gwalior. The front of the gate of Mahal appears to be something like a palace within the old town and people dwelling all around the mahal. Like Gwalior Fort, the Gujari Mahal also still has those blue tiles intact making it look pretty! There are some artifacts placed within the complex that tourists can get a glimpse of. The next time you are visiting Gwalior, do plan to check out Gujari Mahal apart from the Gwalior Fort.

CHAPTER TWELVE

Rani Padmavati and Raja Ratan Singh

"HER LIFE WAS NOTHING BUT A POET'S IMAGINATION"

Rani Padmavati is the famous queen of the Rajputs. She is still remembered for her boldness and holiness. She is also called Padmini. Rani Padmini or Padmavati was a legendary 13th-14th century Indian queen, who has inspired numerous tales of love and honor since the first reference to her story made by Indian poet Malik Muhammad Jayasi in his Awadhi language epic poem 'Padmavat' in the 16th century. Her life story has been released as a movie in Bollywood.

Rani Padmavati was born in a Hindu Kshatriya family to the King Gandharvsen and Queen Champavati of Singhal kingdom in the late 13th Century. Singhal kingdom falls in present-day Sri Lanka. She was taught *Vedas*by her family. She was also skilled in Indian martial arts.

Padmavati was an iconic beauty. Various types of descriptions were going on in four directions about her beauty. Yuvarani Padmini had a talking parrot called Hiramani. When the time came, the king of Singhal decided to get Padmini married and arranged a Swayamvar to choose a worthy groom for her.

Yuvrani Padmavati

Her father disliked her obsession with the parrot Hira man, and had ordered i t to be killed. While the bird was able to fly away and save its life, it later fell into the hands of a bird catcher who sold it to a Brahmin. Once the Brahmin brought the bird to Chittor, impressed by its ability to talk, the localk ing Ratan Singh purchased it from him. The parrot incessantly praised Padmavati's heavenly beauty, which enamoured the king who decided to embark on a quest to marry the princess.

Raja Ratan Singh and Rani**Padmavati**

The bird guided Ratan Singh and his 16,000 followers to Singhal, which they reached after crossing the seven seas. The king began 'Tapasya' in a temple which Padmavati visited after being informed by the parrot, but she left the temple without visiting him and regretted her decision once back in the palace.

Ratan Singh, who was about to immolate himself after learning that he missed t he chance to meet the princess, was stopped by deities Shiva and Parvati who advised him to attack the royal fortress. He and his followers, still dressed as ascetics, were defeated and imprisoned, but as the king was about to be executed, his loyal bard revealed that he was the king of Chittor.

Gandharv Sen agreed to marry Padmavati to Ratan Singh and also arranged 16,000

'padmini' (most desirable) women for his companions. As he began the return journey, the Ocean God created a devastating sto4rm8 to punish him for his arrogance in winning over the most beautiful woman in the world.

As they finally reached Chittor, Ratan Singh, who was already married to Nagmati, witnessed a rivalry between his two wives. After getting married to Raja Ratan Singh, Padmini arrived in Chittor as Rani Padmavati. All the people were surprised by her beauty. Raja Ratan Singh appointed

a special team of w orkers to serve Rani Padmavati. He began to take

care of her without any deficiency.

The marital life of Rani Padmavati and Raja Ratan Singh was a delight. One day, Raja Ratan Singh exiled a Raj Purohit named Raghav Chaitanya on the charge of treason. Raghav Chaitanya reached the court of the Sultan of Delhi, Allauddin Khalji, and described Padmavati's exceptional beauty.

"RANI PADMAVATI SHOWS HER FACE TO ALLAUDIN KHILJ IN A MIRROR"

Then Raghav Chaitanya joined hands with Sultan Allauddin Khilji of Delhi to take r evenge on Raja Ratan Singh. He awakened the lustful desires in the mind of Allauddin Khilji by describing the beauty of Rani Padmavati in many ways. Allauddin Khilji was fascinated on the Maharani Padmavati and came to Chittor to s ee her.

At first, Raja Ratan Singh and Rani Padmavati were not ready to meet Allauddin Khilji, but to avoid war for such a silly cause, Rani Padmavati agreed to show her face in the mirror. Allauddin Khilji became completely enamoured by looking at the beautiful face of Rani Padmavati in the mirror. To get her he arrested King Ratan Singh in a fraudulent way.

Allauddin Khilji agreed to release Raja Ratan Singh on the condition that Rani Padmavati sleeps with him one night. Rani Padmavati sprinkled cold water on his lowly dream. Using her intellect, she released Raja Ratan Singh from imprisonment of Khilji. Allauddin Khilji got angry with this and declared war on Chittor directly.

Determined to obtain Padmavati, Khilji laid siege on Chittor, but when Ratan Singh offered him tribute to save his wife, he captured him by deceit after feigning a peace treaty. At Padmavati's behest, Ratan Singh's loyal feudatories Gora and Badal reached Delhi dressed as Padmavati and her companions to free him, and while Gora was killed in a fight, Badal escorted Ratan Singh back to Chittor.

While Ratan Singh was imprisoned, a neighbouring Rajput king, Devpal had made advances to Padmavati. When Ratan Singh returned to Chittor, he decided to punish Devpal for his misdemeanour. This resulted in a single combat duel between Ratan Singh and Devpal during which they killed each other.

War continued for many days. The soldiers of Raja Ratan Singh could not fight for a long time against the powerful army of Allauddin Khilji. All possibilities of defeat of the Rajput army were close at hand. Raja Ratan Singh was murdered in the battle field by the enemy, King Devpal who was also attracted to the beauty of Rani Padmavati. Finally, Allauddin Khilji succeeded in his mission.

Rani Padmavati got worried after hearing the news of Raja Ratan Singh's death. She did not want to surrender her heart and body to Allauddin Khilji. Rani Padmavati concluded that it is better to die happily instead of suffering in his hands. That is why she decided to do Johar or self- immolation. Before the arrival of Allauddin Khilji, according to the custom of Johar Rani Padmavati jumped into the huge fire and sacrificed her life. Thousands of Rajput women who lost their husbands in the battle gave up their life with Rani Padmavati.

In the meantime, Allauddin Khilji invaded Chittor again, following which Nagmati and Padmavati committed self-immolation (sati) on Ratan Singh's funeral pyre, with the other women of the fort committing mass self- immolation (jauhar) to save their honour.

JAUHAR

(SELF –

IMMOLATION)

Allauddin Khilji was deeply disappointed when he came in after the death of Rani Padmavati. Inspite of winning the war, Allauddin Khilji failed to get Rani Padmavati. Respect is more is more important than life, this is the great life lesson to be learned from Rani Padmavati.

Rani Padmavati is still respected by the people of Rajasthan. The beautiful Queen Padmavati of Chittor is worshipped for the sacrifice made by her. She is a figure of p atriotism for the people of India.

Padmavati Jauhar

Jauhar was an ancient Hindu tradition performed by Rajput women who wanted to avoid getting into the hands of the enemy. They performed ceremonial self- immolation after confirming her husband's death in a battle.

After the death of Raja Ratan Singh, Rani Padmavati was left with no choice to escape the evil intentions of Allauddin Khilji and save the esteem of Chittor but to sacrifice herself. The famous Chittor Jauhar comprised King Ratan Singh's first wife too, along with all the women of Chittor.

The Padmini Mahal, where Rani Padmini or Padmavati lived, is considered pious in Rajasthan. In her memory, various temples and shrines have also been built in Rajasthan.

जौहर-

CHAPTER THIRTEEN

Emperor Jahangir and Nur Jahan

"THE MUGHAL QUEEN WHO WIELDED THE MUSKET"

The fourth Mughal Emperor Jahangir finally found 15 years of wedded bliss with his twentieth wife , Nur Jahan. This is the story of how a woman from a Persian immigrant family fallen on hard times used not only her looks, but also her intelligence and shrewd c ommon sense to become the most powerful woman of her time

Nur-ud-din Mohammad Salim, born on August 31st, 1569, was Emperor Akbar's eldest s urviving son and heir, later to bec ome Emperor Jahangir (World Conqueror).

Prince Salim was first married on February 13, 1585 to his cousin Rajkumari Manbhawati Bai, daughter of Bhagwant Das of Amer, the son of Raja Bharmal and the brother of Akbar's Hindu wife and Salim's mother Mariam uz-Zam ani. The Rajkumari was renamed Shah Begum, and two years into the marriage produced a son Khusrau Mirza.

Though Salim w as the heir presumptive from an early age, he was impatient for power and revolted in 1599 against his father Emperor Akbar, who was engaged in a campaign in the Deccan at the time, thus, setting the prec edent for Mughal princes rebelling against their Emperor fathers. Though unsuccessful in his rebellion, he was pardoned due to the influence of powerful court ladies, such as his grandmother Maryam Makani. According to one theory,

Akbar too died suddenly on 3rd October 1605 after a bout of dysentery and on his death-bed named Salim as his successor. Salim ascended the throne in 1605 a s Emperor Jahangir. During the first year of Jahangir's reign, his eldest son **Khusrau**led a failed rebellion against him. However, Khusrau's forces couldn't fight the might of the Mughal Empire and he was defeated and brought to Jahangir bound in chains. The father did not show clemency as Akbar had done towards him and had his own eldest son blinded and thrown into prison. The emperor also had 2000 rebels executed, so it was a bloody start to his 22 year long reign.

Jahangir's reign proved to be strong and stable, and he was successful in consolidating the Mughal Empire. Like Akbar, he too was religiously tolerant, but was beset with a growing addiction to alcohol and opium that later was to leave him in a be fuddled state.

Emperor Jahangir is celebrated for his patronage of the arts, architecture, and culture, and was a keen horticulturist, botanist, ornithologist, bird watcher and even interested in the sciences. His rule saw many advances in these fields. Some of the impressive achievements due to his patronage include Kashmir's Shalimar Gardens, the world's first celestial globe, painter **Ustad Mansur's** methodical documentation of animals and plants, and the advancement of portrait painting through the establishment of a royal studio.

Jahangir married a string of pretty girls from princely Mughal, Rajput, and Kashmiri families. One of his earlier favourites was the Rajput Princess Jagat Gosain Begum, who he renamed Taj Bibi Bilqis Makani upon their wedding in 1586. She gave birth to Prince Khurram, the future Emperor Shah Jahan, Jahangir's successor. However, Jehangir's twentieth and last (disputed, he may have married five more times

according to one historian) wife is considered to be the love of his life, who w considerable power over his heart and his realm.

ielded

Nur Jahan, *nee*Mehr-un-Nissa, was born in Kandahar, present-day Afghanistan, into a family of Persian nobility and was the second daughter and fourth child of a well b orn couple who had fallen on hard times in their homeland. At the time Mughal India had a thriving, robust and prosperous economy that attracted immigrants looking for a better life. One such was an impecunious Persian aristocrat Mirza Ghias Beg. Taking his pregnant wife Asmat Begum and his three young children with him, the young family made the arduous journey from Persia to India on mules.

In 1594, at the age of 17, Mehr-un-Nissa was married by royal consent to Ali Quli Beg Ist'ajlu, also a Persian immigrant, who had been forced to leave his country after the death of Shah Ismail II whom he had served. Ali had joined the Mughal army under Akbar as a companion to Prince Salim. As a reward for his loyalty to the prince, Akbar arranged his marriage to Mehr-un-Nissa, whose family by now was considered a well settled Persian family and was also in the Emperor's employ. Though their union produced no children, Ali had a daughter Ladli Begum from a previous marriage that his young wife doted on and brought up as her own.

One day, on a royal hunt in Bengal, a ferocious man-eating tiger jumped to attack Akbar riding on the back of the elephant. Quick as lightening, Ali leapt up, tossed the tiger off and then slayed it when it fell to the ground. The hero of the day, he earned t he title Sher Afghan (Tiger Tosser) and was made a captain of the Imperial Guard in Bengal by a grateful monarch.

According to popular belief, two years after Akbar died; Jahangir spied the

beautiful M ehru-un-Nissa and sought to add her to his harem. She, however,

spurned the emperor's overtures and was faithful to her husband. Yearning for her, Jahangir had Sher Afghan conveniently killed in 1607 under the cooked- up circumstances of his rebelling against the Governor of Bengal. His widow and daughter were then summoned to court by the Emperor and made ladies- in-waiting to his stepmother, Empress Ruqaiya Sultan Begum, Akbar's first

wife and daughter of the M ughal Prince Hindal Mirza.

Meanwhile, Mehr-u,Nissa's family was not doing so well. Her father, a *diwan* to an *amir-ul-umra*(provincial governor), stood accused of embezzlement and her brother of treason. Under these circumstances, according to the official story, in 1611, while accompanying Empress Ruqaiya to the palace *meenabazaar* (funfair) during the *Nowruz* (New Year) spring festival, Jahangir met the 34- year-old widow, was smitten and immediately proposed. They were married on 25th May. The emperor gave her the titles of Nur Mahal (Light of the Palace) and Nur Jahan (Light of the World) to match his name Nur-ud-Din Jahangir.

Nur Jahan had a piercing intelligence, wit, charisma, a volatile temper, but sound common sense. Soon, winning her husband's trust, she became the most powerful woman in the Mughal Empire then at the peak of its power and glory, no mean feat considering she was barren and didn't produce any heirs for Jahangir.

A fast decision maker, Nur Jahan is considered by historians to have been the real power behind the throne for more than fifteen years sitting alongside Jahangir behind a discreet *jharoka*(overhanging enclosed balcony) to receive audiences. She wielded more power and was granted more honours and privileges than any other Mughal Empress. For example, she was the only Mughal Empress to have coinage struck in her name; not only was she present when the Emperor held court, but even held court in his place when he was absent or indisposed; she oversaw the administration of several *jagir* (land parcels) and consulted with ministers; she was given charge of the imperial seal, and her consent was necessary before any document or order gained legal validity; she was consulted by the Emperor before he issued any orders; she was even decreed a *Nishan,* a privilege reserved for royal males. As his dependence on alcohol and opium grew, so did his reliance on his Empress. Nur Jahan had first her father and then her brother Asaf Khan appointed the Grand *Vizier*(Prime Minister). To consolidate her family's position, Nur Jahan arranged for her stepdaughter Ladli to marry Jahangir's youngest son, Prince Shahryar and her niece, Asif Khan's daughter, Arjumand Banu Begum (later known as Mumtaz Mahal) to marry Prince Khurram (Jahangir's third son and the future Emperor Shah Jahan). The family's future prosperity was, hence, assured.

Additionally, Nur Jahan was a great huntress. She often accompanied Jahangir on royal hunts and was renowned for her courage, temerity, marksmanship, and boldness. On one occasion, she killed a tiger with her first shot, which even the official royal huntsman Mirza Rustam couldn't do. On another, she is famously reported to have shot down four tigers with six bullets during a single hunt. Jahangir writes, "As a reward for this good shooting I gave her a pair of bracelets of diamonds worth 100,000 rupees and scattered 1,000 *ashrafis* (gold coins) over her."

Nur Jahan was a great philanthropist as well, arranging the marriages and dowries of countless orphan girls and aiding those in need. A woman with many talents, she herself designed lovely outfits, veils, and ornaments, decorated the palaces, and arranged grand feasts and entertainments. She was even a poetess. Persian arts and culture flourished in the land during this time. However, it was her love and the care that she took of the emperor, that won her his heart. He writes, *"I did not think anyonewasfonderofmethanNurJahanBegum"*.

In 1621, when Jahangir fell seriously ill, she assiduously nursed him back to health. Another time, it was Nur Jahan's turn to fall ill, and Jahangir's chief *hakim*(physician) brought her back to health. For this service, Jahangir bestowed on him three villages and his weight in silver such was his devotion to his wife.

The heir to the throne and Jahangir's favourite son Prince Khurram obviously resented his stepmother's undue influence and the fact that it was to her rather than the heir that the emperor turned to for advice. Moreover, Nur Jahan clearly favoured her son in law Prince Shehryar (Khurram's half- brother) to be next in line. When the Persian forces besieged Kandahar, Nur Jahan ordered Khurram to march to save the city, but he refused to follow her orders fearing that in his absence he would lose his position. As a result, after a 45 day siege the gateway city was lost to the Persians for which he was blamed. Tensions mounted even further, erupting in open rebellion by Khurram in 1622. Jahangir's army chased Khurram's rebel troops all over India until he surrendered unconditionally in 1626. The family strife further weakened the emperor's already deteriorating health.

Then, in a dramatic turn of events, in 1626, Jahangir was captured by rebel leader **Mahabat Khan** while the emperor was on his way to Kashmir to recuperate. Quickly organizing an attack on the enemy to rescue the emperor; Nur Jahan herself courageously led one of the units on top of a war elephant that was hit. Surrendering to Mahabat Khan, she too was placed in captivity with her husband. While imprisoned, the wily Empress organized a cunning plan and succeeded in their escape.

Jahangir died aged 58 on 28th October 1627 on the way back near Sarai Saadabad, Kashmir. He was buried in a mausoleum in Shahdara Bagh, Lahore.

A brief war of succession followed in which Nur Jahan's brother Asaf Khan betrayed her in favour of his son in law Khurram. Khurram had his half--brothers Shehryar and the blinded Khusrau executed to leave no possible contenders to the throne. His other half-brother alcoholic, **PrincePervaiz,**was considered too weak and in effectual to be much of a threat. Khurram took the imperial throne of Hindustan and was crowned as the Emperor Shah Jahan.

Though Nur Jahan lost her power and influence at court, she was pensioned off by Shah Jahan with a sum of 2 lakhs and a comfortable mansion in which to live with Ladli Begum. She remained faithful to Jahangir's memory, wearing only simple white clothes, and attending no entertainments. Her only extra vagance was erecting fine Mughal buildings. She first constructed her father's mausoleum, now known as Itmad- ud- Daulah's Tomb in Agra, the first Mughal structure built of white marble. Built on the banks of the River Yamuna, it is said to resemble a silver jewel box placed in the center of a garden and is said to have inspired Shah Jahan's Taj Mahal. She also built Nur Mahal in Sarai, Punjab, and Nur Afshan Garden, Agra. She continued to compose Persian poems under the pseudonym ***Makhfi.***

Nur Mahal BHAVANPUR

Jahangir'sTomb

SHAHDARA BAGH-LAHORE

Nur Jahan died on 17th December 1645, aged 68. Buried in a tomb, she herself had constructed near her beloved husband's in Shahdara Bagh, she had on it inscribed the epitaph:

"On the grave of this poor stranger,
Let there be neither lamp nor rose.
Let neither butterfly's wing burn, Nor nightingale sing."

CHAPTER FOURTEEN

Prithviraj Chauhan and Sanyogita

**"ALL IS FAIR
IN LOVE AND
WAR"**

i thvi raj Chauhan or Rai Pithora was a king from the Chahamana(Chauhan) dynasty. He ruled Sapadalaksha, the traditional Chahamana territory, in present-day north-western India. He controlled much of the present- day Rajasthan, Haryana, and Delhi; and some parts of Punjab, Madhya Pradesh and Uttar Pradesh. His capital was located at Ajayameru (modern Ajmer).

Early in his career, Prithviraj achieved military successes against several neighbouring kingdoms, most notably against theChandela kingParamardi. He also repulsed the early invasions by Muhammad of Ghor, a ruler of the Muslim Ghurid dynasty. However, in 1192 CE, the Ghurids defeated Prithviraj at the Second battle of Tarain, and executed him shortly after. His defeat at Tarain is seen as a landmark event in the Islamic conquest of India, and has been described in several semi-legendary accounts. The most popular of these accounts is Prithviraj Raso, which presents him as a Rajput.

How Píithviíaj Chauhan met Samyukta

Prithviraj Chauhan, the king of the Chauhan dynasty. who ruled parts of present- day Rajasthan, Delhi and some parts of Uttar Pradesh.

Prithviraj is also the last Rajput king to rule Delhi. After that the Muslim conquest of the Indian subcontinent.

Samyukta was the daughter of Jaichand, the King of Kannauj. She was known for her engrossing beauty. Soon, tales of his Prithviraj bravery reached the ears of Sanyogita .

Samyukta who also known as Sanyogita fell in love when a painter from Prithviraj's court, Panna Ray, visited Kannauj. and showed his painting of the king to her. The same painter painted Sanyogita's painting and showed it to Prithviraj. As a result, both fell in love with each other.

Prithviraj Chauhanand Sanyogita

Prithviraj in Sanyogita Swayamvara

PrithvirajChauhangained popularity for his fearlessness and chivalry. Jaichand was jealous of his popularity. Both Jaichand and Prithviraj were from a rival Rajput clan.

As Jaichand heard about the affair of his daughter Sanyogita. Jaichand decided to insult Prithviraj and organised a Swayamvara for his daughter in 1185 CE.

Jaichand invited eligible princes and kings - except Prithviraj.

Love Story of Prithviraj and Sanyogita and Swayamvara

But as Prithviraj was in love with Sanyogita's beauty, he soon came to know about Swayamvara and decided to join that.

When the Swayamwara was proceeding all rajas were rejected by the princess.

Princess Sanyogita

The statue of Prithviraj (as a security guard) build by Jai Chand was chosen by Sanyogita.

Just after that Prince Prithviraj who was hiding came out. Sanyogita put the garland around his neck.

He took Sanyogita up in his arms and whisked her a way to Delhi.

Jaichand allianced with Ghori

Jaichand was in anger and in the mood to take revenge. So, he allianced with Muhammad Ghori, who was against Prithviraj and was previously defeated 16 times, and extended his support to Ghori to attack Delhi.

When Ghori attacked Prithviraj, Prithiviraj lost the war and Ghori acquired him. Legend has it that Prithvi had begun to ignore state affairs after his wedding to Sanyogita.

Love Story of Prithviraj Chauhan and Princess Sanyogita were full of trust, exoticism and fairy tales.

CHAPTER FIFTEEN

Aurangzeb and Hirabai

"A HEARTLESS EMPEROR FALLING IN LOVE AT FIRST SIGHT"

The last great Mughal Emperor, Muhi-ud-Din Aurangzeb, who took the regnal name Alamgir, is remembered as much for piety as he is for craftiness. Some

like t o remember him as an austere, religious and God-fearing monarch, who wanted nothing more in life than to spread the teachings of Islam throughout his vast realm. His detractors, however, remember him as a treacherous and insatiable tyrant, who was ruthlessly Machiavellian in his conduct.

When he was eighteen-years-old Prince Muhi-ud-Din fell head over heels for a Hindu slave girl and gave in entirely to the pleasure of love and pursuit of feminine charms.

The Mughal harem was a secret world behind strictly closed doors. There are very few, if any, recorded stories related to that part of the royal palace. The Mughals r uled for over two centuries as absolute masters, and for a century more as titular heads. Hundreds of girls must have passed through the royal gates destined for the harem - gifted by compliant Rajas, presented by sycophant courtiers, captured in grim battles and gifted by friendly world monarchs. Yet not much is known about how these concubines lived. Precisely how were they were treated? How did they spend their leisure time? How much space was allotted to each? What rights did they enjoy? What privileges were they granted or, indeed, what was their eventual fate? The harem remained a truly forbidden city if there was one.

"DEPICTION OF A YOUTHFUL AURANGZEB LOOKING AT HIRABAI"

Therefore, it is remarkable that the details of this passionate relationship, between a man c onservative prince and a slave girl, have entered the history books through multiple reliable sources. The incident has been mentioned by Niccolao Manucci in his contemporaneous detailed autobiography titled "*Storia do Mogor*" or *Mogul India 1653-1708, vol. I* and by Nawab Samsam-ud-Daula Shah Nawaz Khan in his oft- quoted *Ma'asir al- Umara*. The incident has also been mentioned in detail by Aurangzeb's biographer Hamiduddin Khan Nimchah in *AhkameAurangzeb*, written in 1640.

A PRINCE CLIMBS TO MEET HIS BELOVED – LATE 18TH CENTURY MUGHAL INDIA

There in the garden, Aurangzeb's eyes locked on to one girl who was holding a branch of a tree and humming a tune

Emperor Shah Jahan had personally led his forces to Deccan in 1631. During the campaign, his favourite wife, Mumtaz Mahal, died during childbirth at Burhanpur. She was temporarily buried in the city before her mortal remains were moved to the Taj Mahal in Agra during the year 1648. On her death, the Emperor is famously said to have gone into deep mourning, abandoning imperial duties and with drawing to the confines of his palace.

While retreating from the area in grief, he appointed Aurangzeb, then Prince Muhi- ud-D in and only fourteen years of age, as Governor of Deccan. The Prince set up

ourt at Kirki – he subsequently renamed it Aurangabad – that is 220 km south east of Burhanpur. His maternal aunt Salalı Bano, sister of Mumtaz Mahal, was at the time residing at Burhapur. She was married to Khan-i-Zaman Saif Khan, who had served the Mughals well and is variously described as either the Subedar of Burhanpur or Commander of Artillery.

FANCIFUL MODERN IMAGE OF HIRABAI

Burhanpur is located on the outer bend on the right bank of the River Tapi. In the inner side of the bend was located the village of Zainabad and a garden named Ahu Khana (deer park), the remnants of which still stand in fairly good condition. At this point, the river flows from north-east to south-west towards Surat, Gujarat, where it falls into the Arabian Sea. The area was thickly wooded and a favoured hunting ground for the imperial court.

In 1636, Aurangzeb was travelling to Aurangabad from Delhi and decided to make a stop at Burhanpur to pay respects to his aunt. One day, she arranged a feast in his honour in the Ahu Khana, which was the royal garden. Since Aurangzeb was a member of the family, the ladies of the harem of the Subedar were not in total seclusion. There in the garden, Aurangzeb's eyes locked on to one girl who was holding a branch of a tree and humming a tune. He was mesmerised and dazzled by the sweet melody and striking beauty of the girl. He sank to the ground and then, visibly disoriented, lay down, unable to stand on his feet.

When her aunt was informed about his condition, she was perturbed and came running bare footed. She sat down beside her nephew trying to revive him. After a little while, he regained his bearings. Despite her urging, he didn't disclose the reason for his discomfiture. A despondent and grief-stricken feeling prevailed in the house and the feast was disrupted.

Around midnight, when Aurangzeb was composed enough, he went over to his aunt and told her the reason for his affliction. On hearing about the girl, she became tormented and distraught. She told him that the girl is a dancer and singer by the name of Hira Bai and was called Zainabadi for belonging to a local village of that name. She

lamented that her husband was very harsh, who didn't care much even for the Emperor. She feared that on hearing that Aurangzeb was interested in his concubine, he might respond violently.

ROYAL LOVERS UNDER A TREE – MUGHAL STYLE MINIATURE

Aurangzeb came away saying that he would find another way of getting the girl.

On this trip, Aurangzeb was accompanied by his close friend and confidante Murshid Quli Khan, the Dewan (Chief Minister) of Deccan. He confided in Murshid and asked him for a way of getting the girl. Murshid volunteered to kill Saif Khan, even if it meant a subsequent death sentence for him, to free the girl. But Aurangzeb didn't want to render his aunt a widow and asked him to directly approach Saif with a request to release the girl to him.

Murshid went over to Saif and put forward the request of Aurangzeb. As reported, Saif d idn't object. Possibly he knew the reputation of Aurangzeb as a headstrong and vengeful youth. He asked Murshid to pay his respects to the Prince, and that he would convey his reply through his wife.

Saif came back to his wife and told her about the desire of Aurangzeb and conceded that he was ready to send Hira Bai to the Prince. However, he didn't agree to give the girl as a gift but asked for an exchange. Saif was knowledgeable about Aurangzeb's harem. Perhaps to keep him off, he told his wife that in Aurangzeb's harem, he was not particularly interested in the daughtero f Shahnawaz – meaning Dilras Begum, the senior consort of the Prince – but would exchange Hira Bai for Chattar Bai, a concubine of Aurangzeb. Caught between two hot headed persons, the aunt demurred in taking this rather humiliating exchange offer but Saif forced her to go on pain of death.

Young Aurangzeb

The aunt called for her palanquin forth with and proceeded to visit Aurangzeb

with the news. Aurangzeb was elated.H e

said that he would send not one but both these girls, one of them being his lawfully wedded wife. He conveyed to his staff to send the girls immediately with his aunt so that he could get Zainabadi without any delay. In the end, only Chattar Bai was dispatched. When the aunt conveyed Aurangzeb's reply, Saif said that now no excuse remained to deny Aurangzeb's desire and sent Hira Bai to him.

Hirabai was a girl of immense beauty a sultry enchantress, a femme fatale, enough to melt a heart. We do know that Aurangzeb, who had a reputation for being religious, lost himself to this girl – the only time it was to happen in his long life.

It is recorded in contemporary resources that Aurangzeb was extremely pleased and merry in the company of his love. He even lost some of his extremist or puritanical leanings. Once Hira Bai offered him wine and asked him to drink to prove his love for her. He took the cup and was about to sip it, but the temptress took it away and said that she never intended for him to drink. Another account mentions that he had started drinking in her company. Certainly, he had started enjoying music and dance during that time.

It is well documented that Aurangzeb and his siblings were extremely resentful against each other. Dara Shikoh was bitter about his brother's haughty and self- righteous attitude. When his spies reported about Aurangzeb's new found love, his exchange of girls with his uncle and, indeed, his interest in music, he went to his father and described the reports in a demeaning manner saying that, "See the piety and abstinence of this hypocritical knave! He has gone to the dogs for the sake of a wench of his aunt's household."

CHAPTER SIXTEEN

Rani Roopmati and Sultan Baz Bahadur

"LOVE GREATLY BLOSSOMED BETWEEN THE TWO"

istorical Mandu is 95 km away from Indore city of Madhya Pradesh (India).

They are historical tourist sites 'Mandu' which is also known as the city of Joy. Mandu used to be the capital of the Paramara Kings of Malwa in the 10th century. It was ruled by the Sultan of Malwa until about the 13th century. It was then named Shadiabad. Mandu is situated at an elevation of about 592 meters from the Vindhya hills. It is the largest fort city in the world. Forts surround this city from all sides. With the arrival of monsoon, the number of tourists starts increasing in many placesof the country and Mandu of Madhya Pradesh is one of such favourite cities..

Rani Roopmati and Sultan

The city of Mandu is adorned with spell-Binding Afghanistan architecture surrounded by baobab trees, native to Africa. The grand palaces are still alive with royal romance while the gateways (darwazas) speak of a history of imperial conquests.

Tragic Love Story of Baz Bahadur and Rani Roopmati

One of the incomplete love stories is in Mandu, a witness to the love of Rani Roopmati and Baz Bahadur. The greenery of Mandu located in Dhar district of Madhya Pradesh and the Roopmati palace here attract tourists from all over the world.

Baz Bahadur was the Sultan of Malwa who inherited the province after the death of his f ather Shujaa't Khan, a governor under Sher Shah Suri. It is noted that in 1555 he declared himself independent and it was during this time only he met his lady love while out on a hunting expedition.

One day when he was out for hunting, a musical tune reached his ears amidst the wild trees and shrubs. The Sultan slowly went in the direction of the tune only to come across a stunning she pherdess singing along with her group of friends. She was none other than Roopmati, the Sultan's future wife. Being, a woman of rare charm, Baz Bahadur fell instantly in love with her soon after getting mesmerized by her exceptional beauty and captivating voice.

He, however, didn't force Roopmati for submission but asked her hand in marriage and requested her to accompany him to his capital. Roopmati being a woman from the lower strata could not say "no" to her Sultan, however, laid her own condition, that, the Sultan would have to construct a 'palace for her' right within the sight of River Narmada. The Sultan readily agreed to the wish of his love and thus was raised the famous Rewa Kund reservoir of Mandu, only to fulfil Roopmati's fancy.

Even today, it is one of the most visited spots of Madhya Pradesh. Those who tour Madhya Pradesh do make it a point to witness this beautiful set which the lover constructed for his lady love.

Palace of Rani Roopmati built by SultanBaz Bahadur

After the construction, the two then married with great pomp and honour both in Muslim and Hindu style. Love blossomed between the two greatly. While,

Rani Roopmati was a great reciter, poetess, composer, and singer, Baz Bahadur was negligent towards his kingdom. He paid no attention to his kingdom and from a Sultan gifted lyricist and musician. They were so involved with each other that they could hardly s tay away from each other – neither in the day nor during the night. This soon transformed Baz Bahadur into a musician and lover. Meanwhile, the news of his laxity towards his kingdom had reached the ears of Akbar and so was the tale of Roopmati's beauty to his General and foster brother Adham Khan.

MUSEUM IN MANDU,
LOCATED AT:- MADHYA PRADESH.

The Heartbreaking Twist

It was Friday, the twelfth day of Rajab, year 968 of the Hegira and 1561 of the Christian Era when the Mughal troops led by Adham Khan attacked Malwa. Baz Bahadur reached Sarangpur with a very small army to challenge the huge Mughal army. However, when he felt that he would be defeated and killed, he then fled from Mandu leaving his harem, province and most prominently his love, Roopmati all alone.

When Adham Khan got to know about Baz Bahadur's escape he tried to lay his hand over Roopmati. However, Rani Roopmati being a lady of great chaste continued to be faithful to her lover even till the last unlike Baz Bahadur who fled away. When she realized that Adham Khan would capture her soon and disgrace her, she consumed poison and set herself free from any disgrace.

Appreciating her loyalty for her husband, Rani Roopmati was buried with respect by Mughal General Adham Khan. Baz Bahadur yet again captured Malwa but for a very short period of time as Emperor Akbar invaded the area. Post that, he wandered in the forest and the mountains for a short period and then submitted himself to Mughal Emperor Akbar. Next, he was made mansabdar in Akbar's Government.

Mandu darshan is incomplete without seeing the palace of Rani Roopmati. This palace, situated

on a 365 meter high rock, was built by Baz Bahadur for Rani Roopmati. Simultaneously, it was also used as a better place for soldiers to monitor the security system of Mandu. In Mandu, Baz Bahadur built a palace on high stone rocks for Rani Roopmati.

Hindola Mahal - Mandu

The king used to listen to the problems of his subjects while sitting in the Hindola Mahal. This palace, being tilted from one side, looks like a swing when viewed from a distance, hence it is called Hindola Mahal. It derives the name of 'Swinging Palace' from its sloping sidewalls. Superb and innovative techniques are also evident in its ornamental facade, delicate trellis work in sandstone and beautifully moulded columns.

In Hindola Mahal there are several unidentified buildings which still bear traces of their past grandeur. Amidst these is an elaborately constructed well called Champa Baoli which is connected with underground vaulted rooms where arrangements for cold and hot water were made.

CHAPTER SEVENTEEN

Maharani Gayatri Devi and Maharaja Sawai Man Singh

"WHEN YOU FALL IN LOVE, AGE DOES NOT MATTER"

Gayatri Devi was born in the royalty of Cooch Bihar. She was the daughter of Maharaja Jitendra Narayan and Maharani Indra Devi. She was born on 23rd May 1919 in London. She was the perfect example of elegance and style all her life. She celebrated happiness for 90 years and died on 29th July 2009.

GayatriDevi,a renowned name in the history of India. A woman of inspirational thoughts, optimistic, daydreamer is yet admirable to every woman of the country lovingly called **Ayesha.**

GayatriDevi was the personality who lived her life on her principles which one should apply in their daily lives. **Althoughshewasprivilegedbyluckshedecidedto workforthedowntroddensectionsofsociety.Shedevotedherwholelifetohelping backwardclasses.**She also joined the democratic party named SwatantraPartyand became a famous face in the political history of the nation. She led a bright political career.

That was the emerging time of women empowerment and Maharani Gayatri Devi was the fresh face to it. **Shenotonlyhelpedpeoplebypoliticalmeansbutturnedintoa socialreformertoo.**She worked for women's education and opened the first-ever girl's school in Rajasthan with **40studentsin1943**, it was named after her name as **MaharaniGayatriDeviGirls'School,**located in Jaipur. **WhenwelookedinGayatri's life we found that she was an orthodox rule breaker.** Her vision, wisdom, and knowledge always encouraged her to do the betterment of society. She inherited her qualities and firm nature from her great Grandmother (Maharani Chimnabai II) and her honourable mother **(IndiraDevi)**which were prominent ladies of their time.

Rajmata Gayatri Devi gorged herself as the epitome of refinement in London. She always lived a happy and regret free life. Born in London, she did her schooling from Glendower Preparatory School, London and acquired secretarial skills from London School of Secretaries. After six years of courtship with Maharaja Sawai Man Singh II, she became the third consort of Jaipur in 1940. In an interview, she said that she isn't a nostalgic person and preferred living in the present. She believes in doing the best she can when she experiences unhappiness around her. The lady, during her young days, was raised in a carefree atmosphere of India's one of the most relaxed royal families. She had in her a philanthropic streak and was always concerned about the welfare of her folks.

Gayatri Devi fell in love when she was 12 years old with almost a double- aged person who was 21 then. The situation yet was not so much normalized for a woman to marry a person who is twice her age by her own will.

But this was **Gayatri Devi** who despite the differences and solid social opposition, fought for her love and married the love of her life "Maharaja Maan Singh" happily in **May 1940.**

Maan Singh had two wives before which automatically made it a hard task for **GayatriDevi**to adjust in the family. **MaharaniGayatriDevi**tackled all the hardships greatly and proved to everyone that her relationship was strong and worthy.

Unlike the other maharanis, she refused to live in purdah and was remembered as the first woman who advocated liberation of women. She also became a fashion icon.

Sawai Man Singh would spend the entire summer in England and having found a Maharani, who was well-versed with the western culture the Maharaja would socialize with the British and came closer to the British royalty.

The Maharaja's other two ranis had premature deaths, while the first Maharani Marudhar Kunwar had a son, Bhawani Singh and a daughter, the second wife, a niece of the first had two sons, Jai Singh and Prithiviraj.

She ruled as Maharani for just seven years. She was a witness to the era when India b ecame Independent in 1947. She also saw the abolition of princely states and later the abolition of the privy purses.

Overcoming all the difficulties of life Maharani Gayatri Devi was leading to greater heights in her life.

Gayatri Devi's Political life and Outlook

GayatriDeviwasthefirst-everladytohavewontheLokSabhaseatby1,92,909 votesoutof2,46,516whichcreatedamilestoneinIndianHistory.

In1962,when the **People'sLiberationArmy**was launching an invasion on a large scale of India's north-eastern borderlands and Ladakh, they caught Indian troops which were not even properly equipped.

The tension between India and China made parliament a fierce space of debate. Gayatri Devi was the one who took this chance firstly to criticize the government's concealment of time-to-time incursions by China into India for few years. Gayatri Devi's statement to Pandit Jawaharlal Nehru: **"Ifyouhad knownanythingaboutanythingwewouldn'tbeinthismesstoday"** shows her bold and sharp political views.

In 1967, **Maharani Gayatri Devi** once again won elections in her home constituency b ut this time the conditions were not accordingly to her. She had to escape England with her family as the Congress party abolished the privileged status of the royal family. The circumstances became worse when her husband died just after a month.

After that, she was recognized as the **RAJMATA**, the **QUEEN MOTHER**, and Colonel

Bhawani Singh as Maharaja who was the eldest son of **Maan Singh** by his first wife.

Gayatri Devi was a firm and determined lady. Her habit was to fight even in the worst situations. After the demise of **MaanSingh**, she again took a stand for her third term in **Parliament in 1971** but unfortunately, the royal status was fully unrecognized. **1975**, brought a tremendously tough time to **RajmataGayatriDevi**and **BhawaniSingh**when they got arrested and sent to Tihar jail although there were no major allegations on them. They had to be imprisoned for six months and after that **GayatriDevi**had to be hospitalized for some time.

Gayatri Devi's inner strength supported her to fight for the imprisoner's rights and, she became successful in curbing the purdah system which was prevailing on a large scale and practiced by women in Rajasthan.

Gayatri Devi was counted as the most beautiful woman of that time and people used to believe that her beauty was not an ordinary one to be considered. Her fashion trends were famous nationwide, and **shewas thefirstladywhostartedwearing chiffon sarees.** Gayatri Devi was a sports lover she enjoyed polo a lot and was a fine horsewoman herself.

Her life is remarkable for us as despite her royal privileges she did not choose to live a straight lavish life but decided to work for society, her elegance and charm would affect generations to come. Especially, girls get empowered by her story. **Assheneversteppedbackwhatever hurdles came in herlife.**

Rajmata Gayatri Devi was an ace equestrienne and an excellent Polo player. She had been associated with polo since childhood when polo more than a sport was a way of living. The first polo match she was in 1933 in Calcutta. Ever since then her ambition was to be a syce. She was chief patron of Jaipur Riding and Polo Club during her later years. After her death in 2009, she and her quintessential polo skills were honored by'Rajmata Gayatri Devi Memorial Cup' sponsored by Rambagh Palace, Jaipur and 'Maharani Polo Cup' celebrated every year in Argentina. She broke the traditional restrictions back in 1962 and bagged a seat in the Indian Parliament. With the world's largest majority of votes, 192,909 out of 246,516, she won the constituency in the Lok Sabha elections. Moreover, she had her firm grip on the seat from 1967 till 1971 as the member of Swatantra Party, a rivalry of Indian National Congress initiated by C Rajagopalachari. However, in 1965, then Prime Minister, Lal Bahadur Shastri asked her to join Congress. After the death of her husband in 1970,she became the godmother of Jaipur and got the title of 'Rajmata'. Representing Swatantra Party, she was a formidable opponent of Congress National Party and its public faces, Jawaharlal Nehru, and his daughter Indira Gandhi. However, this relationship between two strong women reached a tipping point when Prime Minister, Indra Gandhi declared Emergency in the country in 1975. Income tax raids occurring all over the country landed Gayatri Devi behind the bars with the accusation of having undeclared gold and wealth. She was held in jail for five months after which she hated Congress even more. After coming out, Gayatri Devi decided to retire from politics and diverse herself completely towards women empowerment and social welfare. In 1976, she published her biography, A Princess Remembers, penned by Santha Rama

The Princess of Cooch, Behar and the Rajmata of Jaipur died a quiet death in 2009 ass he suffered from paralyticileus and lung infection. She was and will always be an epitome of beauty and bravery and will be remembered for her role in transforming society for the better.

She may not figure among the 50 top women of India, she failed to find a place in the list of those who influenced people or politics, yet at one time she was India's best known woman in the world after Indira Gandhi, who was instrumental in cutting down her political career.

She was an ethereal beauty and a legend. She was not only Jaipur's icon, but a woman of substance who was a pioneer in women's education and set up the country's first exclusive public school for girls in Jaipur. It was named after her, Maharani Gayatri Devi Public School, and later the Sawai Man Singh School in Jaipur again in the memory ofher husband.

She would spend time in England with her son Jagat Singh living in her apartment in London. Jagat Singh married the Thai princess Priyanandana and had two children Devraj Singh and Lalitya Kumari. The marriage did not last and there was tension in the f amily.

After the divorce, Jagat Singh died in 1997 and Gayatri Devi first decided not to give a single penny to the grandchildren. However, when the grandchildren came to Jaipur, love for her own blood saw her writing the will in the names of her grandchildren, which was opposed by her stepsons Jai Singh and Prithviraj whom she trusted.

All her life, she along with her stepsons, fought against Brig Bahwani Singh and dragged him to the court of law. It was Bhawani Singh, who in the later part helped her and when she died, she was given a royal funeral. It was Bhawani Singh who built a chhatri (cenotaph) to commemorate her memory at the Maharani Ji Ki Chhatri where she was laid to rest

MAHARANI GAYATRI DEVI AND MAHARAJA SAWAI MAN

CHAPTER EIGHTEEN

Raja Indrajit and Rai Praveen

"CHARMING PARAMOUR OF KING INDRAJIT KNOWN FOR HER POETRYAND MUSIC"

Orchha is a tiny town in Madhya Pradesh (Central India), known for its beautiful palaces, temples, and cenotaphs of the Bundela Kings from 16- 17th centuries. It is also linked to many popular legends and stories that spice its history, and are kept alive in the local ballads and folksongs.

ORCHHA – MADHYA PRADESH

Orchha is famous for its beautiful cenotaphs built along the banks of Betwa river. In India, oral traditions have always been important for keeping alive the local histories. Even today, the Indian myths and legends continue to be preserved through community traditions such as ballads and folksongs.

For example, in the Bundelkhand region, the ballads and nautanki-theatre about the 12th century stories of the brave warrior-brothers Alha and Udal continue to be very popular even today.

"THE BEAUTIFUL COURTESAN PARVEEN RAI"S LOVE STORY"

Indrajit Singh

The second legend about Orchha is linked to Madhukar Shah's second son, Indrajit Singh and his favourite court poet and dancer, Parveen Rai. Emperor Akbar heard about the beauty and singing skills of Parveen and asked Indrajit to send her to Agra to the royal court. Indrajit was in love with Parveen and did not want to leave her, but she convinced him to send her to the emperor. Struck by her strong love for Indrajit, Akbar gave her gifts and sent her back to Orchha.

The story of Indrajit, Parveen Rai and Akbar was written down by the Orchha poet, K eshav Das, in his book "Kavipriya".

Hindi author **Maitreyee Pushpa** had also written about this legend. According to her story, Praveen's original name was Savitri, and she was the daughter of a courtesan called Kanchana from Gwalior. She was invited to Orchha by King Madhukar Shah. The king fell in love with Kanchana and asked her to stay in Orchha. One of the ghats on Orchha river is dedicated to Kanchana. Savitri was a good dancer and was given the title of Praveen Rai. She shared the love for poetry with King Indrajit and the royal poet Keshav Das.

Another version of this story is that Parveen was the beautiful daughter of a blacksmith. When Indrajit saw her, he was smitten and brought her to his palace. Since she belonged to a "lower caste", they could not have a proper wedding. With the help of the royal poet Keshav Das, she learned poetry, studied dance, and became good at both. She wrote the bhakti poetry in "Ramkaleva of Ramchandrika".

Similarly, there are different versions of the story regarding Akbar's curiosity about her. Indrajit's cousin, Pahad Singh, had deliberately told Akbar exaggerated stories about Praveen and suggested that such a beautiful and good dancer should belong to the emperor's court. Pahad Singh wanted the throne of Orchha and hoped that the love-lorn Indrajit will die without Praveen. Indrajit refused to send Praveen to the emperor and an angry Akbar asked him to pay a h uge fine. Praveen convinced Indrajit to let her go. He was disappointed, thinking that his beloved was greedy and wanted to be the concubine of the emperor.

ThehistoricalBackground: The fort of Orchha includes Parveen Rai Palace, also known as Anand Mahal. It was built in the 16th century. Indrajit Singh was the second son of Madhukar Shah, who ruled Orchha during the final years of the 16th century, while his elder brother Rama Shah was part of Akbar's court.

Some of the wall paintings in the Laxmi temple, built under King Bir Singh in the early 17th century show Parveen Rai. Poet Keshav Das lived during the last years of Madhukar Shah, during the reign of Indrajit Singh and during early years of Bir Singh. The legends of Parveen Rai and Indrajit had probably occurred around the end of 16th century. Since Akbar was born in 1542, so he was in his fifties at that time.

CHAPTER NINETEEN

Krishna and Rukmini

Krishna and Rukmini

"THE PARAMOUNT OF LOVE"

Marriage of Krishna and Rukmini

although perfect in all his roles as son, brother, husband, friend,

father, warrior, king, or mentor, Krishna is best remembered as a lover. His relationship with Radha is considered the paramount paradigm of love. But his disarming charm did not spare any woman in Vrindavan and beyond. Everywhere he went, women gave him their hearts and sought him as their husband and lord.

Hindu mythology ascribes an astounding 16,008 w ives to him! Of these, 16,000

were rescued princesses, and eight were principal wives. These eight included Rukmini, Satyabhama, Jambavati, Mitravinda, Kalindi, Lakshmana, Bhadra, and Nagnajiti. Of these, Rukmini is considered the first among equals.

Have you been wondering who was Rukmini to Krishna? Or why did Krishna marry Rukmini when he was in love with Radha?

Daughter of King Bhishmaka, Rukmini was a woman of great beauty. She belonged to the city of Kundinapura in the Vidarbha kingdom and hence was also called Vaidarbhi. Her five powerful brothers, especially Rukmi, sought a powerful political alliance through her marriage. Rukmi was particularly interested in forging a match between his sister and Shishupala, the prince of Chedi. But Rukmini had long given her heart to Krishna.

Vaidarbhi's first brush with Krishna's magical charm occurred in Mathura. A face-off between the arrogant Rukmi and Balarama became the backdrop of a romance for Rukmini. Krishna, whose tales of beauty and valour she had grown up hearing, was suddenly a reality and she fell in love with the dark cowherd prince. But the occasion made her brother an avowed enemy of the Yadava princes.

A farcical swayamvar

When the time for Rukmini's marriage came, a *swayamvara* was organised. However, it was no more than a farce as Rukmi had ensured

that only Shishupala w ould emerge victoriously. Rukmini was livid at the

idea of such treachery, and would never accept it. She resolved to marry only Krishna or drown herself in the palace well. That was how the Krishna and Rukmini love story took off. We talk about the Radha Krishna love, but the love story of Krishna and Rukmini is no less intense.

She wrote a secret letter to Krishna and sent it to him through a trusted priest named Agni Jotana. In it, she declared her love for Krishna in no uncertain terms and implored him to abduct her.

She suggested that they have a *rakshasa vivaha* – a frowned upon yet recognised form of Vedic marriage where the bride is abducted. Krishna smiled in acknowledgement.

Taking charge oflove

In sending off that love letter to Krishna, Rukmini took two path-breaking steps: one, against the patriarchal system of 'arranged marriage' and two, for the cause of her heart. In a milieu, when women were supposed to be coy (that still hasn't changed!), Rukmini's move was most radical! How could Krishna not respond to this brave call of love?

On the morning of the *swayamvara,* Rukmini made a customary visit to the temple of goddess Katyayani. Seizing the opportunity, Krishna swiftly lifted her on to his chariot and made a getaway. Those who came after them met arrows of the Yadava army waiting at some distance. But an angry Rukmi did not relent and continued to chase Krishna's chariot. Vasudev almost let loose his fury on him but was stopped by Rukmini,w ho pleaded him to spare her brother's life. Krishna let him go with just a humiliating head shave.

Once back in Dwarka, Rukmini was welcomed by Devaki and the others, and a grand wedding ceremony was held. A recitation of the 'Rukmini Kalyanam' is considered auspicious to this day.

Krishna proclaimed that she was goddess Lakshmi incarnate and would forever be by his side. He blessed her with the name 'Sri' and said, henceforth, people would t ake her name before his and call him Sri Krishna.

Rukmini started her life as the first consort queen of Krishna, although she would not be the last.

The drama of elopement would not be the last in Rukmini's life either. A few years into t he marriage, Rukmini got disconsolate because she did not bear any children. Only when Krishna prayed to Lord Shiva, were they blessed with a son, Pradyumna – an incarnation of Lord Kama. However, by a strange twist of fate, the infant Pradyumna was snatched from her lap and reunited only years later.

If parting from her child wasn't bad enough, Rukmini soon had to contend with a string of co-wives. But whenever the question has been raised who was Krishna's favourite wife, everyone has known the answer is Rukmini.

But Rukmini always knew this part of the deal: Krishna could not belong to anyone, not to Radha, not to her. He had to answer the prayers of all who sought him.

As the Paramatma, he had to be everywhere and with everyone at once. Rukmini, however, remained steadfast in her devotion to her lord. Two instances offer proof of her undying love for Krishna.

Not a joke

Once, to ruffle her complacent feathers, Krishna teasingly questioned her choice of a husband. He said she had made a mistake by choosing a cowherd over the many

princes and kings, she could have chosen. He even went so far as to suggest she rectify her 'mistake'. This fake proposition reduced Rukmini to tears and made Krishna realise just how much the thought of not being by his side pained her. He sought her pardon and made things right.

But it was in the instance of *tulabharam* (weighing by scale) that showcased the true extent of Rukmini's loving devotion. Once her chief rival, Satyabhama, was incited by the sage Narada to give away Krishna in charity. To win him back, she would have to give Narada Krishna's weight worth in gold.

An arrogant Satyabhama thought it was easy and took on the challenge. Meanwhile, a mischievously complicit Krishna sat on one side of the scale, watching all proceedings. Satyabhama put all the gold and jewellery she could lay her hands on the other side of the scale, but it did not budge. In despair, Satyabhama swallowed her pride and begged Rukmini to help. Rukmini readily stepped forth with just a *tulsi* leaf in hand. When she placed that leaf on the scale,it moved and finally outweighed Krishna. The strength of Rukmini's love was there f or all to see. She was, indeed, the first among equals.

Krishna and Rukmini were devoted to each other

"DEVOTED TO EACH OTHER – KRISHNA AND RUKMINI"

As compared to the enigmatic Radhaor the fiery Satyabhama, Rukmini's character is relatively docile. Her story begins in youthful defiance but soon matures into a model of wifely devotion. Though not as widely recognized as Radha, Rukmini's marital status grants her love legitimacy – something of great worth in civil society. Despite Krishna's many marriages, she remains firm in her love and loyalty. Rukmini surely had to be a goddess to be able to do that, for no ordinary woman would be able to love like that. Like Sita, she becomes the ideal spouse in the realm of Indian mythology and is reverentially worshipped as Rakhumai alongside her Lord, Vitthal, in Maharashtra.

CHAPTER TWENTY

Moomal and Mahendra

"AN IMMORTAL RAJPUT LOVE STORY"

valentine's Day celebrates the spirit of true love. But love has been an eternal

emotion that transcends all barriers. One such love story from the annals of India's history is the love story of **Moomal and Mahendra**. The vast and diverse landscapes of India have been witness to the inexorable march of time and history.

They have stood as mute witnesses to invading armies, rampaging marauders, devious traders, and the ilk. The mountains, rivers, forests, and deserts of India have watched silently the valour and bravery displayed on Indian terrain, they have also watched in horror, the deceit,slaughter, arson, and destruction.

But amidst all the strife and struggles that the history of India is strewn with, there have been glorious chapters of joy and jubilation, peace, and harmony. One of the most fascinating aspects of Indian history has been t he many stories of love and romance which are so poignant and touching that they are sure to leave one moist- eyed.

These lovers from the many known and unknown pages of history never k new about Valentine's Day. But what they knew was true love, the kindof love for which they were ready to kill and be killed. A love that transcended the frontiers of time and space, love without boundaries, without barriers.

Kak Mahal in Rajasthan where Moomal lived

In these modern times, love is celebrated in the form of Valentine's Day but the love of these lovers from Indian history needs no celebration and is alive even today. If you visit the places where these immortal love stories got carved in the sands of time, there is a chance that you may get to hear the soft whispers of the lovers.

The desert sands of Rajasthan have been sprayed with the blood of many a valiant Rajput warrior. The land is replete with the stories of heart-stirring bravery and valiant battles. But the arid desert has also been the place where exquisite flowersof love have bloomed. One such touching love story is the story of Moomal and Mahendra.

Rajasthan Folk Singer

When walking through the ramparts of the Jaisalmer Fort, a heart-rending folk song often reaches one's ears. It will be a Rajasthani folk singer was singing a very popular ballad that told the tale of tragic love. The story was that of the passionate love of Moomal and Mahendra.

Moomal and Mahendra may not be as well-known as the legendary couples like Romeo and Juliet, Shirin, and Farhad, etc., but the love story of Moomal and Mahendra is as poignant and heart-rending, if not more.

Moomal was a princess who stayed in a Palace known as Kak Mahal with her sisters. She was exceptionally beautiful, and the tales of her beauty were heard far beyond the boundaries of Lodhruva. Lodhrruva or Lodrawa was the capital of the then ruling Bhatti dynasty. It is today a village situated about 15 kilometres from Jaisalmer in Rajasthan, India.

Deserts of
Rajasthan

Fate or the power of love brought a young man who was the prince of Umerkot (in present-day Pakistan) to the Kak Mahal. Sparks flew, hearts fluttered, and love blossomed. Legend has it that Mahendra who was the Prince of Umerkot kept his rendezvous with the love of his life Moomal by riding a fast camel every evening from Umerkot to Lodhruva and returning by morning.

One fateful night circumstances beyond his control ensured that Mahendra did not reach Kak Mahal and the lovelorn Moomal was distraught. Her sisters tried to cheer her up. She so missed her lover, that she asked one of her sisters to dress up like him and go to bed with her.

Mahendra reached Kak Mahal in the wee hours of the morning and was crest fallen to see the figure of a man in bed with his beloved Moomal. Tears sprang to his eyes, he seemed to have lost his senses, as he turned around and galloped away on his camel in a daze. In the gravity of the moment, he forgot the stick he usually carried,

As the sun rose over the Kak Mahal, Moomal opened her eyes from a troubled sleep. Her eyes immediately fell on Mahendra's stick. In a flash, she realized what had happened and became desolate. She waited for her lover but knew deep down that he would not come back. Her grief at the separation from Mahendra was unbearable and she decided to end her life by flinging herself into a burning pyre.

CHAPTER TWENTY-ONE

HELEN OF TROY AND PARIS

"BROKE ANOTHER PROMISE. NOW I BROKE ANOTHER HEART. BUT I AINT TOO YOUNG TO REALIZE, THAT I AINT TOO OLD TO TRY.....TRY TO GET BACK TO THE START."

e story of Helen of Troy is one of the most dramatic love stories of all time and is said to be one of the main reasons for a 10-year war between the

Greeks and Trojans, known as the Trojan War. **Herswasthefacethatlaunched athousandshipsbecauseofthevastnumberofwarshipstheGreekssailed toTroytoretrieveHelen**. She was the most beautiful woman in the ancient Greek world, the daughter of the King of the Greek Gods, Zeus, and the wife of the Spartan King Tyndareus, Leda; or perhaps Tyndareus himself and the goddess of retribution, Nemesis, who gave Helen to Leda to raise. Helen had two (twin) brothers, Castor and Pollux (Polydeuces). Pollux shared a father with Helen and Castor with Clytemnestra. There are various stories about this helpful pair of brothers, including one about how they saved the Romans at the Battle of Regillus.

Helen was so beautiful that she attracted many men from close as well as afar as they not only fell for her beauty but also saw her as a means to the Spartan throne. The first likely mate of Helen was Theseus, the hero of Athens, who kidnapped Helen when she was still young. Later, Menelaus, brother of the Mycenaean King Agamemnon, married

Helen. Agamemon and Menelaus were sons of King Atreus of Mycenae and were therefore referred to as Atrides. Agememnon married the sister of Helen, Clytemnestra, and became King of Mycenae after expelling his Uncle. In this way, Menelaus and Agamemnon were not only brothers but brothers-in-law, just as Helen and Clytemnestra were sisters-in-law.

The most famous mate of Helen was Paris of Troy, but he wasn't the last one. Paris (also known as Alexander or Alexandros) was the son of King

Priam of Troy and his Q ueen, Hecuba. Due to being rejected at birth, he lived

the life of a shepherd on Mount Ida. During the course of his life as a shepherd, Paris was approached by three goddesses, Hera, Aprodite, and Athena who asked him to award the "fairest" of them t he golden apple that Discord had promised one of them. He was offered a bribe by each one of them, but the bribe offered to him by Aphrodite appealed to Paris the most. It was a beauty contest, so it was appropriate the Goddess of Love and Beauty, Aphrodite, had offered Paris the most beautiful woman on earth to be his bride. That woman was Helen, who unfortunately was taken as she was the bride of the year t he Spartan King Menelaus.

ABDUCTION OF HELEN

HELEN WITH KING MENELAUS

Whether or not Menelaus and Helen loved each other is unclear, but later on they may have reconciled. It so happened that when Paris came to the Court of Menelaus as a guest, her beauty aroused an uncontrollable desire in him and in the "*Iliad*," Helen takes some responsibility for her abduction. Menelaus accorded Paris a warm welcome and hospitality, but when he later discovered that Paris had taken off with Helen and other prized possessions for Troy, he was enraged at this violation of the laws of hospitality. Paris was unwilling to return Helen although he offered to return the other prized possessions, but this was not acceptable to Menelaus as he wanted Helen too.

Enter Caption

Before Menelaus won out in the bid for Helen, all the leading princes and unmarried kings of Greece had sought to marry Helen. Before Menelaus married Helen, Helen's earthly father, Tyndareus extracted an oath from these, the Achaean leaders, that should anyone try to kidnap Helen again, they would all bring their troops to win back Helen for her rightful husband. When Paris took Helen to Troy, Agamemnon gathered together these Achaean leaders and made them honor their promise. That was the beginning of the Trojan War.

According to the version presented by Homer in his Iliad, an epic poem written sometime in the 8th century BCE, a massive army of many Greek states sailed for Troy and laid siege to the city until Helen was recovered.

The Greeks imagined this war to have occurred sometime in the 13th century BCE, what we call today the A egean Bronze Age.

A conflict between Mycenaeans and Hittites may well have occurred and archaeologists are mostly in agreement that the great city with impressive defensive walls which has been excavated in modern-day Turkey is indeed Troy. The city has many layers of history and what archaeologists call Troy VI, which dates to 1750-1300 BCE, is regarded as the most likely candidate for Homer and Helen's Troy. A war over trade, resources, and colonies seems quite likely, though not on the scale of the Trojan War.

According to the story, the Trojan War lasted 10 years and took place at the city of Troy in Anatolia. Troy had massive walls and so the war was mostly a siege with some breaks for open warfare on the plains outside the city. Priam, the King of Troy, and his son Hector, both treat Helen respectfully during the conflict, with Hector blaming Paris as the bringer of war. In this period, Paris and Helen had four children, three sons: Bunomus, Aganus, and Idaeus, and one daughter: Helen. All three boys died when a roof collapsed in the chaos at the end of the war.

DUEL BETWEEN MENELAUS AND PARIS

One of the many memorable episodes of the war is when Menelaus battles Paris in a one-on-one fight, with the victor being promised the hand of Helen. Menelaus gets the best of better of the Trojan prince but he is saved by Aphrodite and whisked from the battlefield back to the safety of the chambers. The Greeks do finally win the conflict through the ruse of the Trojan Horse, a massive wooden idol inside of which were hidden Greek warriors who got inside the city and opened the gates for the rest of the Greek army to get f ollow. The Trojans were either all slaughtered or enslaved, a brutal reminder in myth of the folly of adultery. Paris is killed by an arrow fired by Philoctetes. Menelaus, meanwhile, is reunited with Helen.

THE TROJAN HORSE

According to some versions of the story, the Spartan King first draws his sword and intends to strike down Helen before seeing her naked breasts, having a rethink, and then embracing her. Menelaus and Helen then return to Greece, stopping off at various places along the way. Next arriving in Egypt, the couple spends many years there. Unable to get any favorable winds to return home, Menelaus makes trips to Cyprus and then the City of Sidon in Phoenicia, land of fine textiles and silverware, some of which the Spartans received as souvenirs. Next is the trip to North Africa (Libya), and then a trip to Ethiopia as Menelaus treasure trove grows. These Mediterranean detours may have an explanation in the transferal of ideas in art and pottery.

THE BURIAL SITE OF MENELAUS AND HELEN

Rather at odds with her standing in Greek literature, Helen was worshipped as divine at certain Greek sites. Scholars are broadly in agreement that Helen must have first been a goddess and then a semi-divine human figure. It may be that the myths of her abductions were an explanation of the goddess's temporary absences from her cult sites. At Rhodes, Helen was associated with fertility, trees, and vegetation, while at Sparta, she represented the aspects of erotic desire and beauty which Aprhodite similarly represented. One of the oldest sanctuaries dedicated to Helen was at Therapne, near Sparta. Locals believe that Menelaus and Helen were buried at Therapne.

CHAPTER TWENTY-TWO

ROMEO AND JULIET

"OH ROMEO, ROMEO WHEREFORE ART THOU ROMEO? DENY THY"

This story is based on the life of two real lovers who lived and died for each other in Verona, Italy in 1303. William Shakespeare is known to have discovered this tragic love story in Arthur Brooke's 1562 poem entitled "**TheTragicalHistoryofRomeoandJuliet**." Romeo and his friend hear of a party and resolve to go in disguise. Romeo hopes to see his beloved Rosaline at the party, but instead he meets Juliet and instantly falls in love with her. However, Juliet's cousin, Tybalt recognizes the Montague boys and forces them to leave just as Romeo and Juliet discover their love for one another.

Romeo is so deep in love with Juliet, that he keeps lingering near the Capulet house to talk with Juliet when she appears in her window. The pair declare their love for one another and intend to marry the next day. With the help of Juliet's nurse, the lovers arrange to marry when Juliet goes for confession at the cell of Friar Laurence. There, they are secretly married.

Following the secret marriage, Juliet's cousin Tybalt sends a challenge to Romeo who refuses to fight. This angers Romeo's friend Mercutio who then fights with Tybalt. Mercutio is accidentally killed as Romeo intervenes to stop the fight. In anger, Romeo pursues Tybalt, kills him, and is banished by the Prince. Juliet is anxious when Romeo is late to meet her and learns of the brawl, Tybalt's death and Romeo's banishment. Friar Laurence arranges for Romeo to spend the night with Juliet before he leaves for Mantua. Meanwhile, the Capulet family are grieving for Tybalt and so Lord Capulet decided to move Juliet's marriage to Paris the next day. They become angry when Juliet refuses to marry Paris, but they are unaware about the secret marriage between Romeo and Juliet.

THE SECRET MARRIAGE OF ROMEO AND JULIET

Friar Laurence helps Juliet by providing a sleeping draught that will make her seem dead. When the wedding party arrives to greet Juliet the next day, they believe she is dead. The Friar then sends a messenger to Romeo to warn Romeo of Juliet's plan and bids him to come to the Capulet family monument to rescue his sleeping wife. Unfortunately, the vital message does not reach Romeo in time due to an existing plague in the town. Hearing from his servant that Juliet is dead, Romeo is grief stricken and in his grief, he buys poison from an Apothecary in Mantua. He returns to Verona and goes to the tomb where he surprises and kills the mourning Paris. Romeo consumes his poison, resulting in his death. Meanwhile, Juliet arises from her drugged coma. She comes to know what has taken place through Friar Laurence, but she refuses to leave the tomb and stabs herself. The Friar returns with the Prince, the Capulets, and Romeo's lately widowed father.

The deaths of their children lead the families to make peace, and they promise to erect a monument in memory of Romeo and Juliet.

THE MONUMENT OF ROMEO AND JULIET

CHAPTER TWENTY-THREE

Isabelle and Ferdinand of Spain

"A KING DOESN'T HAVE RELATTIVES, JUST SUBJECTS"

Ferdinand and Isabella were one of the most famous power couples in European history. They had an incredibly modern relationship in many ways, with Isabella on an equal par with her husband. They enjoyed a profound love and mutual respect in their relationship, tirelessly working together to achieve t heir aims.

In Ferdinand and Isabella's estimation, their crowning achievement wasn't expanding their empire to include the New World, or uniting the various dominions that would become modern Spain. They believed their greatest accomplishment was driving out all Muslims from their country.

Ferdinand, the son of King John I of Aragon, married Isabella, the daughter of King John II of Castile, on the morning of October 18, 1469. At this time many areas of the Iberian peninsula had been ruled by Muslims for over 700 years. Spurred on by their fanatical religious beliefs, Ferdinand and Isabella were determined to unite their land under exclusively Christian leadership and waged a long, bloody campaign to oust the Moors. In January 1492, they finally achieved their goal and conquered the last Muslim stronghold.

MOORISH SPAIN

It was during Ferdinand and Isabella's watch that the dreaded Inquisition commenced. It became the accepted method for testing the orthodoxy of Jews or Muslims who'd converted to Christianity rather than face banishment from their homeland — or worse. The Inquisition was to have a profound effect on Spain and its people for many centuries to come.

Queen Isabella had a keen interest in expanding Spain's commercial interests wherever possible, even overseas. It was Ferdinand and Isabella who agreed to sponsor a sea captain named Christopher Columbus on an expedition across the Atlantic. This wasn't the first time Isabella had been involved with such an expedition. Spain had claimed the three largest Canary Islands 15 years earlier with the Queen's backing.

The Spanish age of discovery was in full swing when Columbus came back to Spain in 1493 after exploring several Caribbean islands. Between 1500 and 1502, the Crown authorized 12 new expeditions to the area, which included Columbus' fourth and final voyage.

Isabella and Ferdinand are known for completing the Reconquista, ordering the expulsion of Muslims and Jews from Spain, for supporting and financing Christopher Columbus's 1492 voyage that led to the discovery of the New World by Europeans, and for the establishment of Spain as a major power in Europe.

Katherine of Aragon, daughterof Ferdinandand Isabella, jilted wife of Henry VIII.

Back home in Spain, Ferdinand and Isabella shored up their defenses against France, who was their primary enemy by signing treaties with England, the Holy Roman Emperor Maximilian I, and the Habsburgs. They married two of their four c hildren into the Habsburg family, who ruled much of Europe, a wise dynastic move that would play a part in Spain's great rise during the coming decades. Their daughter, Catherine of Aragon, would become the first of the six wives of the future King Henry VIII.

Isabella and Ferdinand

Isabella and Ferdinand ruled much of what is now modern-day Spain for thirty years. Their marriage united the kingdoms of Aragon and Castile and expanded their holdings to continents that until recently were completely unknown. Although they did not accomplish the complete unification o f Spain, by the time they died, their country was well on its way to becoming the most powerful in E urope.

CHAPTER TWENTY-FOUR

Cleopatra and Mark Anthony

"ETERNITY WAS IN OUR LIPS AND IN OUR EYES"

together, bound together by a fusional love, Cleopatra and Mark Antony will accomplish great things:

They re-founded the great **Lagid** kingdom (the name of the immense kingdom of Egypt of one Alexander the Great's former general, the Pharaoh Ptolemy I Soter) by taking over Syria, Cilicia, and southern Asia Minor.

Thanks to the political skill of Cleopatra and the iron fist of Mark Antony, Cyprus was taken over by Egypt from Rome.

They wage war against the Parthians and obtain the allegiance of Armenia and Medea.

Despite his forced marriage to Octavia, the sister of the important Roman consul Octavian, Mark Antony spends all his time with the woman he loves, Cleopatra. Six children will be born from this union.

From their first meeting begins one of the most famous love stories in the world, but also one of the most tragic.

Thanks to his many military triumphs, Mark Antony became one of the most popular men in **Rome** and the favourite of the senate. Unfortunately, his popularity makes him an enemy of the ambitious **Octavian.**

Civil war breaks out. Despite his numerical superiority and more seasoned troops than his opponent, Mark Antony does not manage to achieve victory.

It is finally at the naval **battleofActium**that the couple's fate is sealed. On one side are the fleets of Octavian and Agrippa (a general of Octavian very experienced in maritime battles) and on the other side are those of Mark Antony and Cleopatra. The battle of Actium is bitter and violent, the two sides confront each other in intense collisions colouring the sea in red.

Finally, Mark Antony and Cleopatra are defeated and flee each with their fleets to Egypt. During his escape, Mark Antony is caught in a sudden storm and reaches Egypt much later than his lover.

The battle of Actium is one of the most famous in antique history. It marksthe beginning of the Roman Empire (with Octavian as the first Roman emperor)

Upon his arrival, a rumour is circulated that Cleopatra had not endured defeat and had taken her own life. Mark Antony is overwhelmed by grief and decides that if he cannot live with her in this world, he will join her in the other. So, he takes up his sword and literally throws himself on.

Unfortunately for Mark Antony, Cleopatra's death was on

decides to t ake her own life. As her enemies approached, she asked one of her servants to discreetly bring her a basket of figs, in which she will have previously hidden a **snake.** Cleopatra plunges her hand into the basket, **gets bitten** and dies.

Thus ends the most tragic romance of antiquity.

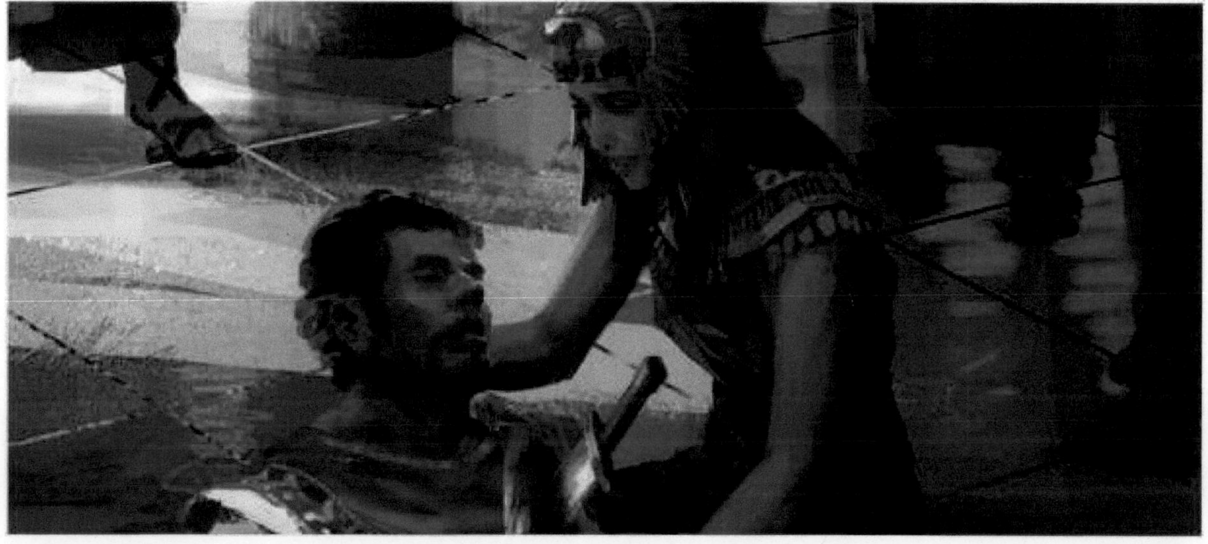

After his defeat in Actium and the presumed death of his lover, Mark Antony feels doubly defeated. He prefers to die by his own hands to join the woman he loves, rather than fall into those of hisenemies.

Examples Of Romance In Art

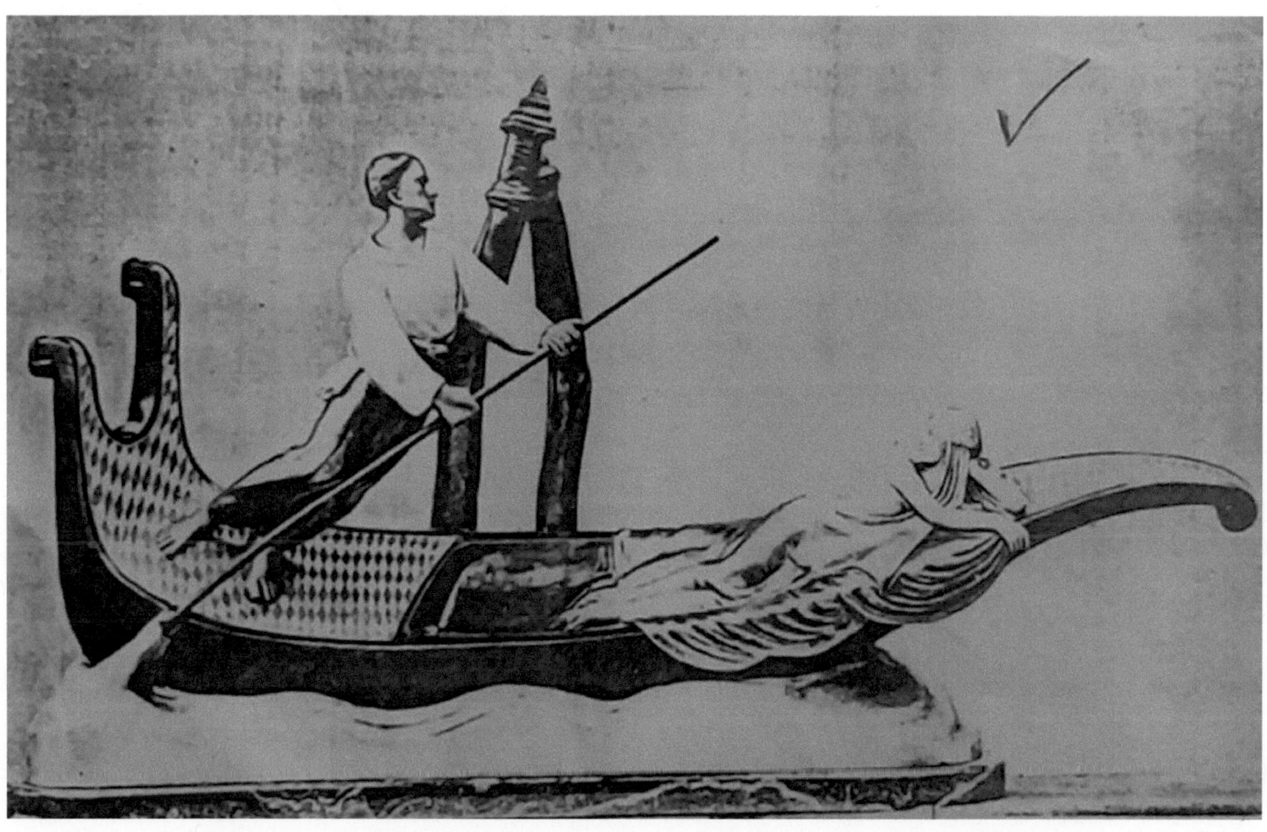

鈴木春信画

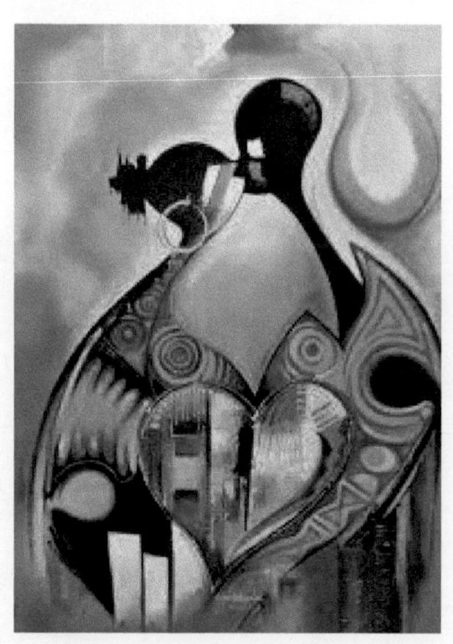

Printed by Libri Plureos GmbH in Hamburg,
Germany